JAMES REANEY

by Ross Woodman

Canadian Writers Number 12
New Canadian Library

McClelland and Stewart Limited
Toronto/ Montreal

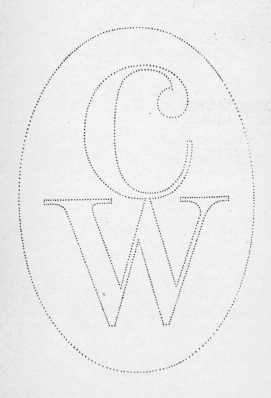

CANADIAN WRITERS

A SUBSERIES
IN THE NEW CANADIAN LIBRARY

Canadian Writers is a series of handbooks
designed to provide the student and general
reader with compact and inexpensive
introductions to significant figures on the
Canadian literary scene. Each book is
written expressly for the series by an
outstanding Canadian critic or scholar and
provides, besides a comprehensive critical
approach to a given author, useful
biographical and bibliographical
information.

NEW CANADIAN LIBRARY
Malcolm Ross, Editor-in-Chief

CANADIAN WRITERS
W. David Godfrey, Editor

© 1971 by McClelland and Stewart Limited

The Canadian Publishers
McClelland and Stewart Limited
25 Hollinger Road, Toronto 374

CONTENTS

To
D.C. Mc.

1

LIFE & ART

INTRODUCTION

For John Hirsch's production of James Reaney's *Colours in the Dark* at the Avon Theatre during the Canadian Centennial year at the Stratford Festival some one hundred and twenty props were required. In certain respects the play might be considered a series of improvisations upon a set of props, as indeed was *One Man Masque* performed unrehearsed by James Reaney for two nights at Hart House Theatre in April, 1960. "*Colours in the Dark* might best be called a play box," Reaney wrote in his Introduction to the play. He went on to explain: "I happen to have a play box and it's filled with not only toys and school relics, but also deed-boxes, ancestral coffin plates, in short a whole life. When you sort through the play box you eventually see your whole life–as well as all of life–things like old Sunday School albums which show Elijah being fed by ravens, St. Stephen being stoned."

The masque-like play, in addition to being a series of improvisations upon a set of props (largely gathered from the Reaney attic), is also a series of improvisations upon a set of poems written over a period of twenty-five years and incorporated, largely unrevised, into the play's text. "Antichrist as a Child" was first published in 1947 in *The Undergrad* at the University of Toronto; "The Sun Dogs" first appeared in *Canadian Forum* (June, 1948); "The Royal Visit" first appeared in *The Red Heart* published in 1949; "The Storm" first appeared in *The Varsity* (January 18, 1960); "Orange Lilies" first appeared in *Twelve Letters to a Small Town,* published in 1962; the poem on Existence, a poetic statement of the theme of the play, first appeared in an as yet unpublished play, *Ignoramus*; *The Dance of Death at London, Ontario,* a large section of which is staged in the play, was first published in 1963. These and other poems function in the play much as songs do in a musical comedy and, covering as they do the entire history to date of Reaney's career, point up the extraordinary consistency within the pattern of his imaginative growth.

The play is loosely structured, held together by such apparently casual devices as a colour spectrum as randomly put together as a child's colour selection in a crayoning book (which is what Reaney had in mind). The looseness is an attempt to image the memory reassembling a life into an imaginative pattern that, as in all Reaney's plays, frees it from the fallen conditions of time and space. "The theatrical experience in front of you now is designed to give you that mosaic-all-things-happening-at-the-same-time-galaxy-higgledy-piggledy feeling that rummaging through a play box can give you. But underneath the juxtaposition of coffin plate with baby rattle with Royal Family Scrapbook with Big Little Book with pictures of King Billy and Hitler—there is the back-bone of a person growing up, leaving home, going to big cities, getting rather mixed up and then not coming home again but making home and identity come to him wherever he is. The kids at the very end of the play manage to get their lightning rod up and attract the thunder that alone can wake the dead."

Reaney's subject in *Colours in the Dark* – "the back-bone of a person growing up" – is the subject of all his work to date beginning with an early novel, *Afternoon Moon*, written and rewritten between the ages of sixteen and nineteen. In that novel, part of which was published (again with revision) in *Here and Now* (May; 1948), Reaney juxtaposes two worlds, one almost entirely fictional, the other largely autobiographical. The autobiographical world describes, under a slight disguise, his life from early childhood on a farm outside Stratford to his decision to enter the University of Toronto, a period also covered (though also extended) in *Colours in the Dark*. The purely fiction world is constructed around the figure of Charles Newburgh, a homosexual aesthete born of Beardsley's drawings and Reaney's early limited understanding of the world of Oscar Wilde. Charles provides in the novel a demonic image of an aesthetic view of life to which the young hero, Albert, is initially attracted, but which, as the novel unfolds, becomes more and more sinister and life-destroying. The first section of the novel, dealing with Charles's homosexual attraction to Albert and Albert's innocent response, is marred by a thoroughly contrived exoticism that stands as a barrier to that actual world upon which the mature Reaney was to impose an imaginative shape. Reaney in *Afternoon Moon* had not yet invented those rites of passage which release his later heroes from the paralysis of an arrested growth. His imagination had not as yet shaped a poetic identity which, for Reaney, is the true "home" for man. Thus he begins his unpublished novel by declaring himself "an exile from the paradise of childhood" and views his life on earth as "a continual retreat" that will one day leave him "free to go back to the Heaven that he has lost."

Constructing a poetic image of himself, Reaney in this early novel too often adopts the imagery and style of the Beardsley *art nouveau* school, thus, by implication at least, identifying his hero with the figure of Charles whom in the novel he ultimately rejects. "I am the Luna-moth fluttering lost and despairfully in the yellow waters of the Sun who is a candle I cannot ever reach," the hero laments. "My pen is the mouth of the moth that tastes even the microscopic perfumes of precious gems: the acrid scent of diamonds, the cinnamon odour of amethysts." The result is an incongruity between the lower middle-class evangelical rural world of the hero's childhood and youth and the Beardsley-like exoticism with which Reaney invests it. The fir tree that grew beside Albert's farm house is "like a black pagoda" and the tiger lilies in the ditch beside the house are "strange immigrants from Cathay." The flattened car tires of his teacher's Buick are "like the great black breasts of blackamoor ladies suddenly shrivelled with senility." The principal at Stratford Collegiate is "an apocalyptic demon on the watch for people who could be dragged down to his den and strapped."

As his vision matured, Reaney's early sensational and artificial exoticism, while still very much present in his work, was put to a better, more organic, use. In *Afternoon Moon* it is essentially decorative; in the later work it images those demonic forces which seek to destroy life and growth. In *Afternoon Moon*, the young hero is clearly "half in love with easeful death;" the narrator sings a dirge on the death of childhood and youth. The difference between the conclusion of this early novel and *Colours in the Dark* is the measure of Reaney's growth as a writer. In *Colours in the Dark* the sick man-child locked up in the dark room of time and space is restored to imaginative life; his blindfold is removed and he walks out into the sun. In *Afternoon Moon* he remains the "Afternoon Moon, a pale white eyebrow rising unheralded and setting obscurely in the hell of the sunset."

ROSS WOODMAN
University of Western Ontario
January, 1970

I

Reaney's literary career was initially an attempt to make imaginative sense out of the various props provided by the accidents of his birth, family and environment. He was born on a farm outside Stratford on September 1, 1926 to parents of Irish and Scottish descent. His father's ancestors came from Ulster where as Protestants they belonged to the Church of Ireland. Upon their arrival in Ontario they identified themselves with the Presbyterians. His mother's family came from Scotland around 1830 and, although initially Presbyterian, they became, through the conversion of Reaney's great grandfather, Plymouth Brethren. Among the Brethren theological disputes were conducted with a vigour reminiscent of the early years of the Reformation. Caught up in them, Reaney's grandfather broke with the Gospel Hall congregation in Shakespeare, Ontario and sought to unite his family with the Gospel Hallers in Stratford. They were, however, prevented from joining because the minister in Shakespeare refused to provide them with a letter of recommendation. As a result the family was left without a church and, as Independent Gospel Hallers, conducted in their home family prayer meetings and family communion from which many neighbours and relatives were, owing to unorthodox convictions, excluded.

Reaney himself attended in his childhood and youth an Interdenominational Sunday School in the country, which was forced to close because of a lack of attendance, as well as a Presbyterian and a Congregational Sunday School in Stratford. In *Afternoon Moon* he left an account of his experience with what he calls the "Evangelical Tabernacle":

> Since I had been accustomed to spend Sunday practising the piano or walking in the fields or reading a book, now that nearly all of these delightful occupations had been snatched away from me and the grating teachings of an Evangelical Tabernacle substituted, it was with intense nausea that I recall the pale young man who taught the Bible to a class of four in the ill-lit jerry-built room that he, himself, erected in the basement of the Tabernacle.... Now I barely remember anything of what the young man taught me about the Bible, except that he, like Mr. Llewellyn, made the Bible out as being as bigoted, depraved, vileminded and anti-Catholic a work as he was a person. He told us all sorts of tales about nuns and priests, convent wells filled with dead babies, etc. which he would confidentially pour out to us as if they really mattered.... Never-

theless, despite the fact that he was narrow and fanatical, there was a certain charm about that minister's giddiness. One of the last sermons he ever preached was one where he stood before us with a black sheet over himself. As he approached the climax of the sermon, he suddenly ripped off the black sheet and stood clad in a white one.

Although Reaney never accepted as a matter of religious belief the Gothic horrors issuing from the pulpit, he early made them a permanent part of his poetic and dramatic machinery. As a result his own Gothic dramas, which include *The Killdeer, The Sun and the Moon* and *Listen to the Wind,* owe an enormous debt to the melodramatic vision which he first encountered in the evangelical world. They are, in large measure, that world raised to the level of imaginative vision. His fondness for melodrama, his extremely simplified characters that at times merely personify a rather child-like vision of good and evil, his radical reversals in the last act that in their own way are informed with a certain evangelical 'giddiness' are distinctive features of Reaney's drama whose roots are in the religious world of his childhood. "Long before I gave up going to church," Reaney wrote in *Afternoon Moon,* "I had given up my belief in various things the Evangelical Tabernacle held dear. Now I have come to believe in them again but in a dreamier, more poetical fashion."

Reaney's reading of the Bible was, from the outset, influenced by the apocalyptic vision inherent in this evangelical world. In his home were to be found commentaries upon the more apocalyptic books of the Bible such as Daniel and Revelations which interpreted the events of the contemporary world, particularly with reference to the Anti-Christ and Amageddon, as the fulfillment of prophesy. In *Daniel and the Revelation: the Response of History to the Voice of Prophesy,* a book which Reaney read diligently in his youth, its author, Uriah Smith, radically distinguished between the "mystical" and the "literal" interpretations of the Bible, defending of course the "literal."

Another book belonging to the period of Reaney's childhood was *Satan or Christ?* described on its title page as "an allegory representing the conflict now raging between evil and good in the home, in the church, in business, in every walk of life." In this book, copiously illustrated, twentieth-century America is interpreted not in terms of the human scene itself but in terms of Angels and Devils warring for the souls of men. In the end the modern metropolis, both in the text and in the illustrations, goes up in flames and the "apparent supremacy of evil" gives way to the "final triumph of the right." The movement of Satan and his fallen host among the faithful is reminiscent of the movements of Mrs. Shade in *The Sun and the Moon* and Madam Fay in *The Killdeer*, and the "final triumph of the right" is accomplished in a manner not unlike the extraordinary reversals in Reaney's drama. It is clearly with such books and such training in mind that Reaney in *Afternoon Moon* looked "back on a childhood where [he] still believed in the Devil, and still believed that he took the shapes of human beings in order to carry out some of his plots and even to become one's dearest friend or nearest relative in order to carry out an especially wicked design." And the illustrations to such books – in which the Devil is always present – is suggested in his memory in *Afternoon Moon* of "watching the Devil as he glided back and forth between Aunt Geraldine and [his] father one Sunday evening when [they] were all at supper."

It is therefore apparent that what Reaney described in "The Canadian Poet's Predicament" (*UTQ*, April 1957) as "the new sects of the Protestant Left" had a profound influence upon the shaping of his imaginative vision. Reaney's mature vision reveals the influence of an evangelical conception of the world in the clutches of Satan awaiting the inevitable Judgement. Though the vision is essentially secularlized–imagination replacing grace– Reaney himself emerges in his work as a member of a defined poetic Elect whose task it is imaginatively to redeem the times. The prophetic stance which he assumes in his major work resides largely in the Blakean manner in which he wields the elements of a primitive evangelical vision into a more sophisticated literary shape.

One of the things lacking in *Afternoon Moon*, a novel that obviously belongs among Reaney's *juvenalia*, is a vision of childhood rooted in and sustained by the timeless ritual and ceremony of games, a vision which accounts for the masque-like qualities of his later drama. And the reason is not hard to find. There is in *Afternoon Moon* no vision of a genuine community such as is found in Blake's *Songs of Innocence*, a work which later had an enormous influence upon Reaney. Reaney was an only child (he has a brother and sister from his mother's second marriage). His father was, during the years when Reaney was growing up, in a continuous state of uncertain physical and mental health. The farm itself had for an extended period to be rented out to a person able to operate it. As a result, Reaney's identification with the farm was damaged at an early age, though during his father's illness he continued to live and work on it. This disruption from the life of the farm is presented in

Afternoon Moon in a highly distorted self-portrait that like so much in the novel serves to reinforce the unfortunate effects of the hot-house style. "Visitors from the farmhouses about us continually bothered my father and mother as to what I was to be," Reaney's narrator comments, "for I did not work much on the farm and at the only threshing I ever attended, I fainted in fright at the hideous noise of the machine.... My father did not force me to do farm work, did not swear at me, kick at me, tell me daily that 'You don't know nothing,' as, I am convinced, most other farmers would have done, but let me moon about the house, read books and practise music. He was so kind I almost felt ashamed of him."

In the novel, Albert's alienation from the farm conducts to his exotic friendship with Charles. What emerges from his relations with Charles is a parody of the child's imaginative world. Echoing the opening passage of the novel, in which Reaney describes himself as an "exile from the Paradise of childhood," Charles in his first meeting with Albert declares: "You are so lucky to be still so close to childhood. More than anything else in the world, Albert, I want to be a child. To have all the pleasures fresh as you have them or have just had them." To which Albert replies: "You're still not too far away from your childhood, Charles." But Charles does not agree: "No Albert, I'm far away from it. And farther, farther everyday. I wish I had never been born or could have stayed in my mother's womb and watched the world from there as in a movie theatre-gray and black shapes moving back and forth across a tiny aperture. But I couldn't. Something drives me on out."

Charles, who lives and entertains Albert in a room without windows or natural light, has retreated into a womb-like world to remain at the age of twenty-eight, like Eli in *The Killdeer* and Kenneth in *The Easter Egg*, an emotional infant. The natural counterpart of Charles's unnatural enclosure is Albert's garden which he maps out when at last he "began to dislike the artificiality of [Charles's] nature and the affectation and perhaps harmfulness of his ideas." The garden becomes a substitute for the farm, created "as a backdrop, a setting for [his] thoughts." Perhaps the most bizarre object in this garden–the first appearance of a play box in Reaney's work–is a decayed staircase leading in reality no where, though in imagination it was "the visible steps for an invisible coach that might sometimes pass that way."

For Reaney, the avenue of escape from the demonic world of arrested growth is the creative imagination. In Charles, he presents a vision of the diseased imagination which, far from releasing the eternal child (Reaney's symbol of the imagination), merely embellishes its tomb. Charles also has his play box which he describes as his "artificial paradise." It contained many curious objects: "there was a huge dead yellow spider, yellow with black speckles; a small Chinese lantern; *Ondine* by La Motte-Fouqué, and a luna moth in a jar."

Although the avenue of escape is absent in the essentially demonic vision that informs *Afternoon Moon*, its presence is on several occasions anticipated. One of the things that Reaney most feared as a child was the embarrassment of a public baptism. Managing in life to avoid it, he offers in *Afternoon Moon* a fictional account of the threatened event. The amused, detached irony in which the immersion is set over against a longing to join a group of children in the Springbank Amusement Park points up implicitly Reaney's initiation into the art of his maturity, an art in which religious rites are transmuted into games and the world of the Amusement Park (which, as Mome Fair, provides in *A Suit of Nettles* the climactic, poetically defining image) becomes almost a definition of his vision. He concludes his account of the baptism: "As I changed into dry clothes and shoes in a deserted bath house, I wondered if I really had been saved for the call of the world, as symbolized by the shrieks of the toy steam engine, had been so overwhelming, so sweet, so winning. In vain did I struggle to oust that Egyptian pleasure from my mind, and substitute the pleasure of softly, gently *dolce-espressivo* sinking into the thistle-down-stuffed arms and breast of Jesus."

The second letter in *Twelve Letters to a Small Town*, for which Reaney won his third Governor General's Medal, is titled "Instructions: How to Make a Model of the Town." Stratford in this poem has become a children's game, a city of the imagination like the New Jerusalem. The transformation of the town into an imaginative model removes from it all those demonic elements which in *Afternoon Moon* made Stratford a "minor Hell." Reaney, as it were, has harkened to "the shrieks of the toy steam engine." Three years prior to the publication of *Twelve Letters to a Small Town*, Reaney won his second Governor General's Medal with his *Suit of Nettles*. In this satirical treatment of Canadian society the farm on which Reaney grew up has become the microcosm of an entire society, a gay, witty and humane vision of the human community. This development from the limited, demonic vision informing both *Afternoon Moon* and his first volume of poetry, *The Red Heart*, was accomplished in large measure by Reaney's growing awareness of a verbal universe in which the Word is liberated from its enslavement to an evangelical literalness and takes up residence in every act of the imagination. At the age of twelve, Reaney wrote in *Afternoon Moon*, *Gone With the Wind* replaced Hell as the focus of his attention.

But if Reaney during his adolescence turned more and more to fiction, giving to it the same power and authority that he had once given to his evangelical religion, he did not as yet discern its redemptive role. The reason for this is partly perhaps that Reaney had never, in the evangelical sense, experienced himself or thought of himself as "saved." He embraced religion not because it was imposed upon him at home, but because it was the only immediately available material upon which his active and demanding imagination could feed. Reaney at first recognized no redemptive power in fiction because, in part, he had in fact experienced no redemptive power in religion. Interestingly enough, Reaney in *Afternoon Moon* identified the end of his childhood with his discovery that numbers went round in a circle and the alphabet came to a swift and sudden end. The discovery of a universe in an imaginatively unlimited alphabet was to come years later. And that discovery brought with it Reaney's "iconography of the imagination."

At the age of fourteen, Reaney left the one-roomed country school at Elmhurst and went to Stratford Collegiate Vocational Institute. Upon graduation he won an entrance scholarship in Greek and Latin to University College at the University of Toronto as well as a County Scholarship (established by George Drew) which took care of his room and board.

Particularly in his study of Greek the world within the alphabet began to open up to him. He dimly recognized that words transmuted things into thoughts, that the manipulation of words was in fact the shaping of reality into a human form. Word lists became an inventory of the world, the stuff from which a cosmos is made; declensions were the beginning of a structure which grammar brought to completion. He had in fact arrived at his true beginning and recognized, however darkly, what for him had always been the case: that the Word dwelt in his imagination.

Language ultimately released in Reaney the sleeping child which he failed to resurrect in his early work. The farm, which as an imaginative body had always evaded him, was destined to come vividly and completely to life as a verbal structure. In his delightful children's play, *Names and Nicknames* (written in 1961 and produced by John Hirsch at the *Manitoba Theatre Centre* in 1963), the life of the farm in all its seasons and in all its varied activities is miraculously present. No play by Reaney exploits such an extraordinary verbal range, moving as it does beyond the reach of conventional meaning into an onomatopoeia that evokes the entire gamut of animal and even vegetable life. As the title suggests, the play is about names and the abuse of names. Names in the play confer identity as does Adam's act of naming in the Garden of Eden. The identity conferred is not, however, limited to the objects which are named; it belongs primarily to the namer himself. The power to name confers upon Adam his identity as man who is lord of all creation. The act of naming in *Names and Nicknames* is a children's game in which the actual children in the audience are initiated into that creative act that confers identity. It is also Reaney's discovery of his "home" not as a place that he has returned to, but, as he pointed out in *Colours in the Dark*, an identity which attends him where ever he is. The villain of the play, Mr. Thorntree, seeks revenge upon children by robbing them of their baptismal name and substituting for it a nickname which conceals identity. He embodies the perversion of language which, among other things, includes the language of Charles's "artificial Paradise" in *Afternoon Moon*.

The recognition of the latent power of language is the rite of passage which conducted to Reaney's prolific creative activity after the publication of *The Red Heart* in 1949. In that year he received his Master's degree from the University of Toronto and, more important, came under the influence of Northrop Frye at Victoria College. In his graduate year he read *Fearful Symmetry*, Frye's study of William Blake's prophetic vision.

The impact of *Fearful Symmetry* upon the development of Reaney's imaginative vision cannot be overestimated. In the first place it provided him with an archetypal vision of the Bible in which the Logos is equated with the imagination, thus transforming in a comprehensive and systematic way Reaney's earlier evangelical world into a literary one. In the second place, it introduced him to an archetypal approach to poetry by means of which he was able to move beyond the limited scope of a subjective lyricism toward the realization of an epic theme. On the level of the imagination, Reaney, with the help of *Fearful Symmetry*, discovered Everyman in a self that he had formally experienced as alienated from society. And, of course, he discovered the prophetic works of William Blake which, until his reading of *Fearful Symmetry*, had remained for him an impenetrable mystery. *Fearful Symmetry*, in other words, provided Reaney with that long awaited and long delayed "conversion" impossible to achieve in his earlier evangelical experience. Reaney, like Blake before him, became a "literalist of the imagination."

But it was a "conversion" carefully gauged to his own requirements. Reaney at University College cherished his freedom from the narrow evangelical world that earlier surrounded him too much to submit without protest to what at the time he considered the Frye cult at Victoria College. He himself as an undergraduate did not attend Frye's lectures, though the endless discussion arising from them among his friends he could not avoid. Recalling the excitement surrounding the publication of *Fearful Symmetry* in 1947, Reaney wrote in his Editorial to the first number of *Alphabet*: "Those were the months when young men and women sat up all night reading *Fearful Symmetry* which had just come out. I think I have been present at more conversations about the Fall than even Adam could have thrown a certain withered apple at, and assuredly more speculations concerning Leviathan than Job scratched his boils at."

Protecting himself against (among other things) the literary evangelism of his Frye-oriented friends, Reaney throughout this period deliberately cultivated the stance of the *infant terrible*, a stance which bore fruit with the publication of his short story, "The Box Circle", in the mass circulation *New Liberty Magazine* (July 19, 1947). The heated debate that developed across the country over the story of a young man who is confronted in a particularly macabre way with the aborted foetus of the girl he made pregnant provided Reaney with a notoriety that any young author might envy. The best of his early poetry, much of it first published in *The Undergrad* and *The Varsity*, was now brought together in a single volume, *The Red Heart*, and accepted by McClelland and Stewart for publication. Not surprisingly, the volume shares much in common with *Afternoon Moon* and, to its disadvantage, reveals no direct debt to either Northrop Frye or William Blake.

Indeed, Reaney's indebtedness in his first volume of poetry, as well as in "The Box Circle" (first published in *The Undergrad*), is primarily to the kind of religion and the kind of sermon vividly portrayed in *Afternoon Moon*. And yet with a difference. In the May, 1948 number of *Here and Now*, Hugh Kenner contributed an article, "The Case of the Missing Face", in which he argued that the time had come for Canadians to forego their "pathological craving for identification with the subhuman", look into a mirror, and, however unpleasant, shape an honest image of what they found there. Both in the poems and in the short story, Reaney was mirror-gazing on a more than personal level. He was, in Kenner's phrase, conducting "a new raid on the inarticulate", and particularly on that distinctively Southwestern Ontario neurosis whose chief symptom is an almost pathological fear of psychic exposure. By constructing an image of the Canadian as he knew him (which included himself) he was in his own manner bringing a people to judgement. And the cries of indignation (which on some level was music to his ears) were the cries of the damned. Reaney's own controlling image of himself in this first phase of his literary career was that of the Antichrist hiding his hooves in a pair of ill-fitting shoes. It is an image he never entirely dropped, though his later reading of Blake brought him to that genuinely transforming realization that all true poets are of the Devil's party. In that knowledge lay the release of his epic and dramatic powers, both of which he pursued with the beguiling innocence of a sly serpent.

II

With the completion of his M.A, and *The Red Heart* accepted for publication, Reaney left for Winnipeg in 1949 to teach, among other things, creative writing at the University of Manitoba. It was in this course, of which John Hirsch and Tom Hendry were informal members, that Reaney first began to apply some of the writing techniques suggested to him by his reading of Northrop Frye. His writing assignments included, for example, presenting in their contemporary forms the four Zoas of Blake's unfinished epic and the retelling of fairy tales in a manner that incorporated the student's conception and experience of modern life. He himself began work on *Night Blooming Cereus* as a libretto for an opera by John Beckwith, completing the first version while teaching summer school at Acadia University in Wolfville, Nova Scotia in 1952.

Night Blooming Cereus grew out of Reaney's friendship with Pamela Terry and John Beckwith at the University of Toronto. Beckwith, a student at the Conservatory, was interested in drama (he acted in a student production of *Pride and Prejudice*) as, of course, was Pamela Terry. After the publication of *The Red Heart*, Beckwith set to music Reaney's "Great Lakes Suite" which was first performed on the CBC in 1950 with Lois Marshall as one of the soloists. It was on the basis of that music that Reaney in the composition of his libretto was able to work out the elaborate syllabic patterns to conform with Beckwith's style. The experience made him much more aware of prosody and at least partly accounts for the technical sophistication of the verse forms in *A Suit of Nettles*.

Night Blooming Cereus was, in reality, Reaney's first attempt at a form of drama that shares many of the features of an archetypal masque in which the various phases of an individual life are related to a larger mythic pattern. Most of Reaney's plays have much in common with the kind of opera represented by, for example, Mozart's *Magic Flute* and the kind of play represented by the late romances of Shakespeare, *The Tempest, Cybelline* and *The Winter's Tale.* What interested him were magical transformations that allowed eternity to break through a linear, logical, timebound structure to reveal a brazen nature in its original golden form. Experimenting initially with a libretto, Reaney in *Night Blooming Cereus* was free to focus more intently upon sheer word play and sound patterns such as he had found and enjoyed in Edith Sitwell's *Facade* and, above all, in Mother Goose Nursery rimes.

The success with which Reaney incorporated the world of myth, fairy tale and nursery rime into his dramatic vision is the result of his conscious effort to shape his mature vision upon the recovery and recreation of childhood. Like Wordsworth's in *The Prelude* that recovery had sometimes less to do with the memory than it had to do with the imagination. The world that Wordsworth thought he was recalling was, at least in part, a world he was creating. Like the rustics described by Wordsworth in his Preface to the *Lyrical Ballads,* Reaney's characters belong essentially to a pastoral world. He, like Wordsworth, is a "Sylvan historian." And, like Wordsworth, he was not always aware of this fact; it was indeed his growing insight into the nature of literary modes that allowed to his imagination greater and greater autonomy. With that growing autonomy Reaney found himself more in the tradition of Blake and Yeats than in the tradition of Wordsworth. Significantly enough, when he returned to Toronto in 1956 to begin work on his Ph.D. he registered immediately in Frye's course on literary symbolism (out of which emerged Frye's *Anatomy of Criticism*) and chose as his thesis topic a study of Spenser and Yeats. No Canadian writer has managed more successfully than Reaney to fuse the poet and the scholar to the benefit and enhancement of both.

Reaney's love of nursery rimes and fairy tales was, from the outset, directed to a dramatic end. In the living room of his farm house outside Stratford home-made marionettes acted out the world of Mother Goose and the brothers Grimm. Reaney has recalled that one of his favourite radio programs was *Let's Pretend* which, initiating from New York during the thirties, presented every Saturday morning dramatizations of Grimm's Fairy Tales. Walt Disney was a childhood hero; when *Fantasia* was first shown in Toronto he travelled over a hundred miles by bicycle to see it in the original uncut version. Still his favourite movie is *Snow White and the Seven Dwarfs* (though he has seen *Great Expectations* thirty-four times).

This magical world of fairy tale and nursery rime, a world of pure *mythos* and simplified characters compressed and refined "like gold to airy thinness beat," had, with its intensity, imagery smash, sudden transition and concrete symbols that defy interpretation, much in common, stylistically and technically, with the evangelical vision of life that also captured his youthful imagination. By equating the two worlds according to the criteria of poetic faith, Reaney was able to endow evangelical religion with some of the characteristics of an Amusement Park and bring to the rides, shows and games of an Amusement Park some of the characteristics of evangelical religion. The two worlds are present in Mrs. Shade and Madam Fay, both of whom reveal in their actions the curious blend of evangelist, circus barker and side-show performer.

In Reaney's libretto to *Night Blooming Cereus* can be seen the beginning of the second phase of Reaney's career, a phase in which he brought together the varied activities of his childhood within the larger framework of an archetypal vision celebrating re-birth. The setting is the village of Shakespeare, Ontario, and the story tells of the return of a grandchild in search of her grandmother whose life is rooted in an evangelical faith purged of its grosser elements. But it is also a fairy story that has something in common with *Little Red Riding Hood* as well as a pastoral romance in which the magical night-blooming Cereus bursts into its once in a hundred years bloom when the grandmother first touches her granddaughter. Finally, as Reaney's detailed stage directions suggest, it is also in part a marionette show. The grandmother's two-roomed house is described by Reaney in terms of a child's game of cards. One card has a door, another card has water basin with pail and dipper, yet another card has a stove.

As Reaney had earlier learned to play games with language, he was now learning to play games with live actors (an extension of his earlier marionettes) on a stage. And it was a redemptive game he was now playing. "Surely," wrote Reaney in his Introduction to *Colours in the Dark*, "one of the things theatre could be about is the relaxed awareness that comes when you simply play . . . Life could be an endless procession of stories, an endless coloured comic strip, things to listen to and look at, a bottomless play box." He then went on, describing the rehearsals for the Stratford production: "I suppose that in the

Age of Dread in which we live this may seem to some foolish. I disagree. At rehearsals I have felt that (and the rehearsals were in my high school auditorium with a great many teachers of mine looking down from portraits) here was such a peaceful kingdom, energetic, joyful and serene—it made the world of dread much easier to face afterwards."

For Reaney the entire experience of theatre is the creation of a "peaceful kingdom" which is indeed the Kingdom of God viewed as a kingdom within, itself the image of a little child. Thus the demonic world of one version of *The Killdeer* suddenly dissolves when Rebecca takes Madam Fay's hands and gives her the world she has always wanted. The stage direction reads: "She grabs hold of Madam Fay's hands and whirls her around and around with her. Like two children playing at spinning they laugh and enjoy themselves." At the conclusion of *The Sun and the Moon*, Andrew Kingbird forsakes the demonic world of Mrs. Shade not because he was able to penetrate its evil but because, as he says in the last lines of the play, "I suddenly remembered that my music examination was tomorrow and that I really should be practising for that, shouldn't I ?" At the conclusion of *The Easter Egg*, Kenneth miraculously recovers when Polly restores to him a glass egg from his childhood play box. "And I suddenly knew I could talk and act once more," he declares. *One Man Masque* ends with one of Reaney's loveliest lyrics, "The Lost Child," which concludes:

Oh life in Death! my bonny nursling
Merry drummer in the nut brown coffin,
With vast wings outspread I float
Looking and looking over the empty sea

He finds the cradle by the coffin and rescues it, saying the last lines kneeling like a shepherd at Christ's Cradle.

And there! in the—on the rolling death
Rattling a dried out gourd
Floated the mysterious cradle
Filled with a source.

I push the shore and kingdom to you,
O winter walk with seed pod ditch:
I touch them to the floating child
And lo! Cities and gardens, shepherds and smiths.

Reaney's six years in Winnipeg were for him in some respects a period of exile. When *The Red Heart* appeared in 1949 it received there scant recognition. It was not reviewed, for example, in either of the Winnipeg papers. The *Manitoba Theatre Centre* had not yet been formed; the richly rewarding relationship with John Hirsch had not yet developed. In 1951 he returned East during the Christmas break and married Colleen Thibaudeau in St. Thomas, Ontario. Colleen Thibaudeau was in the same year as Reaney at University College, a member of the small literary group on the campus and, even then, one of the finest lyric poets in the country. To her poetry she brought an extraordinary verbal felicity and imagistic power, as well as an uncanny ear for rhythm and sound patterns partly developed by her reading of French poets such as Mallarmé and Valery (she studied French poetry with the Canadian poet, Robert Finch). Her range was narrower, though more polished, than that of Reaney whose larger scope she recognized. Her background was Irish and Acadian French, and, like her husband, she had Ulster ancestors. Her early environment was free thinking, agnostic, politically committed. Reaney had enormous respect for her poetic taste, and the growing ease, playfulness and joy that informed his lyrics after *The Red Heart* owe much both to her presence and her influence. Reaney's marriage to Colleen Thibaudeau played a part, and an important part, in the opening and maturing of his poetic vision which, in his case, was so closely identified with his immediate and actual life. Both *Afternoon Moon* and *The Red Heart* offered an essentially negative vision of love, marriage and family. After his marriage, his work became more and more a celebration of them. Their first child was born in 1952 and named after both the father and the grandfather.

In 1956 Reaney returned with his wife and two children to Toronto to take his Ph.D. and, in a record time of two years, completed the course work, the general examinations and the thesis. During his years in Winnipeg he returned each summer to the East and, of course, became caught up in the miracle at Stratford. His growing interest in drama was nourished not only by the renaissance in his home town but also the composition of *Night Blooming Cereus* and *A Suit of Nettles* which he worked on during the Winnipeg years. In essence *A Suit of Nettles* is a pastoral modelled on Spenser's *Shepherd's Calendar*, yet in its portrayal of rural life and its use of dialogue it is essentially dramatic in form. Upon completion of the thesis in the spring of 1958, Reaney turned at once to the writing of *The Rules of Joy*, which was the title he gave to the first version of *The Sun and the Moon*, and in October of that year entered it in the *Globe and Mail Stratford Festival Contest*. It received no award.

Unlike the radically revised version, *The Rules of Joy* was written especially for the Stratford stage. "This play," he pointed out in his Note, "has been written with the Festival Theatre in mind and therefore uses the poetic symbolism and pageantry that theatre's shape demands." The pageantry offers what Reaney again in his Note called "the essence of country life in Ontario as I know it"; it is seen in full measure in the Prologue which includes along the theatre aisles berrypickers, a funeral procession, a store keeper with "an unbelievably long string of children," a choir singing "Shall We gather at the river," and a wedding group. And, again with Stratford in mind, Reaney began his Prologue with the following speech:

> Shall I tell you a story of the jealous Moor or of the old king and his three daughters? No. I shall tell you a story of myself when fifteen years ago I was sixteen. It happened in my father's kingdom. His kingdom was the realm of love where people learnt the rules of joy. I can see that summer in my father's house. Summer in the village, in the church, in the fields, those roads, the people I summon to appear and myself as then out of the lake of time and death–come up!

The major weakness of the unrevised play is that Reaney, far from presenting the "essence of country life in Ontario," focused upon an elaborately melodramatic and thoroughly improbable plot involving the efforts of an abortionist posing as a Christian revivalist to destroy the Reverend Kingbird. The machinations of Mrs. Shade dominate the traffic of the stage, while the pastoral vision is relegated to brief moments of pageantry. In his later plays, particularly in *Names and Nicknames* and *Colours in the Dark*, the decorative pageantry invented by Reaney to exploit the Stratford stage was divested of its artificial splendour and took on the natural vitality inherent in the rural world of Reaney's imagination. There were in addition problems of plot and structure, but the play's real weakness lay in its origin. The fact is that Reaney's imaginative world was not adaptable to the kind of spectacle that momentarily attracted him to Tyrone Guthrie's productions. What Reaney was in search of was not the Stratford stage treatment but the kind of thing he later described in *Alphabet*. "How can those interested in making life better in this country help our drama?" he asked in an Editorial in June, 1962. "There should be a club that does nothing but seasons of plays by Canadians. It should do them in a bare, long room up above a store, probably infested by Odd Fellows or Orangemen on easily avoidable nights. Nobody should have any truck with that grand Bugaboo–Lighting. Five two hundred Mazda watters always turned on will do for any play that lights its own way, as a play should. One thing we don't need right now is 'spectacle', often hiding the play's barrenness.

After completing *The Sun and the Moon,* Reaney returned to Winnipeg to fulfill a two year obligation arising from his leave of absence to complete his thesis. Back in Winnipeg, he began work on *The Killdeer.* Becoming discouraged with his progress, he sent off the first act to Pamela Terry who encouraged him to finish it and then submit it for production by the *Alumni Players* at the University of Toronto. The play, directed by Pamela Terry, was first performed on January 13, 1960 by the *University College Alumnae Society* at the *Coach House Theatre* in Toronto.

The Killdeer showed an enormous advance over *The Rules of Joy.* In the latter play, the fifteen year old hero, Andrew Kingbird, acts as narrator and the entire play suffers from a narrative continuity that is closer to the novel than it is to drama. Reaney had not yet discovered how to foreshorten narrative into the shape of a scene. The play, as a result, is essentially shapeless and the characters, especially Mrs. Shade, tend to describe themselves rather than present themselves. And the descriptions too often attempt a naturalistic explanation of behaviour. Mrs. Shade belongs not to a realistic world but to a world of fairy tale. She is the archetypal witch. As Reaney was to recognize, the power of fairy tale, like the power of the nursery rime, is the unique kind of congruity that emerges when a reader (or an audience) is assaulted by continuous incongruity. The world of the nursery rime and the fairy tale has more to do with being than with becoming. What is required is a "willing suspension of disbelief" that allows the archetypal characters moving in a mythical world to work upon those depths of human nature sealed off from daylight consciousness. Mrs. Shade is a creature of the night being explained by the habitual rules of the day. The more she and others explain the less an audience understands.

In the published version of *The Killdeer*, Madam Fay is allowed a certain "motiveless malignity" and the children of light who are momentarily trapped in her darkness have a lyrical splendour that is its own *raison d'être*. Above all, Reaney had learned in *The Killdeer* what he had not learned in his earlier play: the rules of joy. *The Killdeer* was Reaney's first successful dramatic game to be enacted on the stage.

In addition to *The Killdeer*, both *Night Blooming Cereus* and *One Man Masque* received their premiere in Toronto in 1960. Reaney had completed the first draft of his libretto for Beckwith's proposed opera in 1952 but Beckwith himself was unable to complete the score until some seven years later. He had intended that the short opera should be followed by Reaney reading some of his poems. Reaney instead decided to write for the occasion *One Man Masque*, which was directly influenced by Yeats' "Vision" and Blake's "Mental Traveller." Two years before, *A Suit of Nettles* was published. It was, in many respects, Reaney's finest, most mature, work to date, written with a professional assurance and control that reveal a dazzling technical range. "The poem," Reaney pointed out in his Note to the reader, "was written out of interest in a number of things: geese, country life in Ontario, Canada as an object of conversation and Edmund Spenser's *Shepherd's Calendar.*" Reaney's interest in geese was by no means limited to the actual geese for which as a child on the farm he was temporarily and rather half-heartedly responsible. Goose for Reaney was essentially Mother Goose and, not surprisingly, it is a Goose alphabet that first confronts the reader when he opens a copy of *A Suit of Nettles.* From this cryptic alphabet it emerges that the wanderings of Reaney over the social and other terrains of Ontario are the wanderings of Old Mother Goose "on a very fine gander." Under the letter F, Reaney quoted from *Twelfth Night*: "Let there be gall enough in thy ink, though you write with a goose-pen, no matter." The gall is limited not merely to the matter; it embraces the manner as well; lyrics assume a proper dissonance. "The coat of arms of the Company of Musicians," quoted Reaney under the letter I, "viz., *a swan*, with expanded wings, within a double tressure [the gridiron], counter, flory, argent. Perverted into a goose striking the bars of a gridiron with its foot, and called 'The Swan and Harp," or 'Goose and Gridiron.'"

Clearly evident in both *One Man Masque* and *A Suit of Nettles* was the fusion of Reaney's "formal" and "accidental" education. Blake, Yeats and Spenser, Grimm's Fairy Tales, Mother Goose Nursery Rimes, Walt Disney, the Bible, marionettes, evangelical religion, farm life in Ontario have, among so much else, been hammered into a distinctive imaginative shape: a regional vision devoid of provincialism, its dimensions at once local and cosmic. Blake's Albion was both a lower-middle-class Englishman and universal humanity; his Jerusalem was both London and the Holy City of the Christian visionary. Reaney's "one man" is both a country boy growing up in Southwestern Ontario and an evolving humanity whose essential form is Christ. And Reaney's Stratford is at once a provincial town and the Biblical city in both its fallen form as Babylon and its redeemed form as Jerusalem.

III

In 1960, with his wife, three children, a play box, two Governor General's Awards, three new works on the stage in Toronto and more plans than his alphabet could number, Reaney accepted an invitation to join the Department of English at the University of Western Ontario in a London thirty-eight miles from Stratford, one hundred and twenty miles from Toronto. Physically and psychically he was "home."

Immediately upon settling in London, Reaney mailed out from 17 Craig Street the first number of *Alphabet*, dedicated to what he called "the iconography of the imagination." He had begun collecting the material for the magazine two years earlier in Winnipeg, taken there a night course in printing, and type-set the first number on a printing press owned by the Fine Arts Department at the University of Manitoba.

Like so much in Reaney's career, *Alphabet* was conceived during Reaney's graduate year at the University of Toronto when he first came under the influence of Northrop Frye. The only literary magazine of any major significance in Canada then was *Tamarack Review* (*Canadian Literature* began in 1959). Reaney was dissatisfied with *Tamarack Review* because, run by an editorial board, it lacked, from his point of view, a genuine editorial policy. The evangelical strain, if not the evangelical belief, ran very deep in Reaney and he was eager if not to convert at least to publicize and share a point of view which he considered essential to the shaping of a distinctive Canadian culture. Reaney conceived of *Alphabet* because, like Blake before him, he was eager to build Jerusalem; *Alphabet* was one of the weapons of his "mental fight." Reaney made this perfectly clear in his manifesto printed in the first number.

Perhaps the drive behind this magazine might be found in the following cluster: (a) The most exciting thing about this century is the number of poems that cannot be understood unless the reader quite reorganizes his way of looking at things or 'rouses his faculties' as Blake would say. *Finne-*

gan's Wake and Dylan Thomas' 'Altarwise by owl-light' sonnet sequence are good examples here. These works cannot be enjoyed to anything near their fullest unless one arouses one's heart, belly and mind to grasp their secret alphabet or iconography or language of symbols and myths. A grasping such as is involved here leads to a more powerful inner life, or Blake's 'Jerusalem's wall.' Besides which it's a hell of a lot of fun. It seems quite natural, then, in this century and particularly in this country, which could stand some more Jerusalem's wall, that there should be a journal of some sort devoted to iconography.

The publication of *Alphabet* launched a new phase in Reaney's career, one in which he became more actively involved in the development of a Canadian identity. He was now in a very real sense a "literalist of the imagination" concerned to work directly with groups of people in the building of Jerusalem. The building of Jerusalem was for Reaney a two-fold task: on the one hand the documentation of Canadian life; on the other the subjection of that documentation to the imaginative transformations of myth. Each number of *Alphabet*, accordingly, was to be devoted to a particular myth. The first number was devoted to the myth of Narcissus and Jay Macpherson did the honours. Hope Lee submitted a documentary on identical twins. After listening to her tell stories about her life as an identical twin, Reaney, in his Editorial, said that "it suddenly came to [him] that here was proof that life reflects art. The myth of Narcissus reaches out and touches with a clarifying ray the street scene where the two human beings glide by also in the toils of reflection. That's how poetry works: it weaves street scene and twins around swans in legendary pools. Let us make a form out of this: documentary on one side and myth on the other: Life & Art. Into this form we can put anything and the magnet we have set up will arrange it for us."

Reaney is here describing the imaginative form that his own work was now taking. Using myth as a magnet to assemble his documentary material, he constructed a series of collage-like dramas that brought him finally to a vision of his own life in or near Stratford woven around "swans in legendary pools," himself as Narcissus on the Avon stage.

Reaney's earlier use of the Narcissus myth revealed a purely subjective phase in which, as in the traditional view, the youth pines away and dies for love of, in Reaney's case, his own childhood image. In the later phase, of course, the drowning of Narcissus in the self-reflecting pool becomes a baptism converting, as in *One Man Masque*, a coffin into the cradle of the imagination, at once Christ and the Babe of Blake's "Mental Traveller."

In the July eclogue of *A Suit of Nettles*, Valancy and Anser debate the merits of a traditional and progressive education. Valancy, a traditionalist, defends what the pedagogue, Old Strictus, taught, which strikes the progressive Anser as "useless so far as the actual living of life is concerned." Among the things which Strictus taught were the stones that support Jerusalem's wall. "When I was a gosling he taught us to know the most wonderful list of things," Valancy says to Anser. "You could play games with it; whenever you were bored or miserable what he had taught you was like a marvellous deck of cards in your head that you could shuffle through and turn over into various combinations with endless delight." In *Alphabet*, Reaney sought by means of the building blocks of the alphabet to produce all those various combinations of delight which in their totality constitute Jerusalem. Valancy goes on to tell Anser how at the end of each year the goslings would make themselves huts, lie down on their backs with large stones on their bellies and recite their lists of things forwards and backwards until "they knew all that a young goose was supposed to know." Though Anser considers these lists a "maze of obscurity," Valancy assures him that when the goslings had completed their agony and learned their lists–"the moment when they rolled the stone away and climbed out of their burdock hut"– there was great joy "as if they had been reborn into another world."

In the *Listener's Workshop*, which Reaney began in November, 1966 in the Green Room of the Grand Theatre in London, Reaney assumed the role of a very progressive Old Strictus teaching a group, stretching all the way from children to adults, the joys of metaphor. Working with a few homely props he set the group free to improvise a cosmos. When some of his Satyrday School students decided to establish a centre, which would serve as a workshop for all the arts, they called it the *Alpha Centre* signifying a conviction that all things have their origin in the imagination. In March, 1967, Reaney moved his *Listener's Workshop* from the Green Room at the Grand Theatre to the top floor of the *Alpha Centre* in the old McMartin Block on Talbot Street in London above the Market Drug Store. It was precisely the kind of place that Reaney had had in mind for several years and he set to work to help the group construct an extremely primitive theatre without a stage and without lights, but seating up to sixty persons in a manner that created little or no separation from the actors. When it was finished it looked very much like the jerry-built Evangelical Sunday-School room described in *Afternoon Moon*.

Just as the *Alpha Centre* grew out of the *Listener's Workshop* so the *Listener's Workshop* grew out of *Listen to the Wind*. *Listen to the Wind*, which Reaney considers the most satisfying play he has yet written, was originally conceived as a play about the four Bronte children. Reaney's interest in the Brontes goes back to his childhood; *Jane Eyre* and *Wuthering Heights* were and remain two of his favourite novels. He revised his first draft of the play, substituting a Canadian setting for Haworth parsonage and four Canadian cousins for the four Bronte children. Together the four cousins decide to put on Rider Haggard's *Dawn*, the first novel that Reaney read as a child and one which he has always associated with the world of the Brontes. Thus, though the play as revised has ostensibly nothing to do with the Brontes, it is the sort of thing that Emily, Charlotte, Branwell and Anne would do, and certainly the kind of novel they would read.

In *Listen to the Wind*, Reaney found the form ideally suited both to his talents and to his vision. The adult world is presented in terms of a late Victorian melodrama seen through the eyes of a child. The problem of realism vs. fantasy is therefore avoided; the drama is a midsummer's dream acted out in the enchanted forest of the imagination. A chorus of children take care of the sound effects and provide with their movements most of the props. Reaney in writing it was not struggling to live up to the demands of the Stratford stage; rather, he imagined himself back on the farm outside Stratford with a clean white sheet stretched across the living room where in fact, like Owen, he had first dreamt out Ridar Haggard's *Dawn*.

Reaney in London became more and more interested in children's theatre. Such a theatre, he believed, should not and need not exclude adults. The staying power of nursery rimes and fairy tales depends, he argues, upon the fact that adults enjoy reading them to children. Indeed, Reaney has suggested, children's classics are far more sophisticated and demanding than most so-called adult literature which, by being adult, has lost its belief in metaphor. The children's theatre he had in mind, therefore, was a children's theatre for adults. The adult world of the twentieth century tends, according to Reaney, to take for granted C. P. Snow's notion of the two cultures or, like F. R. Leavis, imposes in the classroom certain moral imperatives upon literature which are alien to the imagination. Metaphor, for Reaney, is its own justification, and those who affirm it for its own sake affirm the true identity-confirming activity of man. The child's world is metaphor and, as such, human and civilized. Every act of the imagination is a recovery of it, a restoration and a rebirth.

Reaney had hoped to make his *Listener's Workshop* a true image of the London community, a place where its psychic life could be acted out even as Owen in *Listen to the Wind* dreams it out. He had not intended to make it an improvisation school for children; rather in founding it he had hoped to attract a group between the ages of eighteen and twenty-two. Children, rather than adolescents and young adults, gravitated toward it because they were less inhibited, were still in possession of a world of metaphor. For Reaney metaphor is man's birthright, a gift bestowed which like Wordsworth's "celestial light" is gradually and inevitably lost. To recover it it is necessary to strip away those delusions of common sense that would persuade men that the imagination is the father of lies. Those who have suffered most from the delusions of common sense—the psychically wounded members of society, park drunks, petty thieves, addicts of various sorts—would be welcomed to the Workshop and in that "bare room" over the Drug Store they would be invited to improvise a lost world in the hope of meeting again some identity-conferring image of themselves: "The Magus Zoroaster, my dead child,/ Met his own image walking in the garden./ That apparition, sole of men, he saw."

In *The Easter Egg*, written in 1963 and first performed in Middlesex Theatre at the University of Western Ontario as a rehearsed reading, Reaney presented the creative process he later had in mind at the Workshop. Kenneth, the twenty-one year old hero, has suffered a traumatic shock that has robbed him both of memory and speech as a result of witnessing his father's suicide. His guardian, Bethal, yet another of Reaney's witches, has, with the support of every plea to common sense, managed to preserve him in a state of oblivion for special reasons of her own. Polly, the good fairy, has, however, nursed him during Bethal's absence back to life by endowing him again with his lost human power, which is to say the power of naming originally given to Adam in Paradise. Polly restores the Word to Kenneth and by the power of the Word he is released from the evil spell which Bethal had cast upon him.

For Reaney the possession of the Word is the granting of eternal life. Those who dream it out, like Owen, awaken like Adam in *Paradise Lost* to find it true. Keats, it will be recalled, compared the imagination to Adam's dream. It is a conviction that Reaney shares. And it is the conviction of an evangelist who, having discovered for himself the meaning of the Word, seeks to build a Kingdom upon it. Reaney in London, Ontario, has imaginatively recreated the evangelical world he knew as a child. His pulpit is the stage; and for a time his church was the *Alpha Centre* and his congregation the members of the *Listener's Workshop*. In the spring of 1968, the Workshop put on the first book of the Bible, a book which his group hoped to dream out to the end.

To his great delight, Reaney has found in London a ready-made community of artists who, in different ways, share his vision. In 1959 John Chambers returned from Spain to London, his home town, and began to paint out the psychic world of his childhood; a haunting portrait of his mother, for example, is called "The Artist's First Bride." Chambers and Reaney worked together on *The Dance of Death in London, Ontario*, the first publication of the *Alphabet Press* in 1963. The press itself Reaney bought in Ayr, Ontario, from the *Ayr News*. It was installed in the Dixon Building close to where Chambers then had his studio. In 1965 Greg Curnoe did the set and marionettes for Reaney's *Little Red Riding Hood* which was shown daily at regular intervals at the Western Fair. Chambers then filmed it. Curnoe himself has helped to impose a vision or form on his city with his figurative and verbal paintings that imaginatively record with child-like precision a scene partly of his own making.

In 1962 Reaney won his third Governor General's Award for *The Killdeer* and *Twelve Letters to a Small Town*. The latter work is a visionary recreation of his home town. In his eleventh letter, "Shakespeare Gardens," Reaney revealed the presence of *The Merry Wives of Windsor* in the Ladies Auxilliary of the Orange Lodge, of *The Tempest* in the violet lightning of a March thunderstorm, of *The Two Gentlemen of Verono* in an elegant gentleman with waxed moustachio on Wellington Street. "It suddenly came to me that here was proof that life reflected art. . . . Let us make a form out of this: documentary on one side and myth on the other: Life & Art." That form is still very much in the making; Reaney has a long way to go before he will be ready to "abjure" his "rough magic."

2

CONVERSIONS OF ANTICHRIST

I

"I can remember about twelve years ago at Toronto feeling the final clutch of the so-called scientific world," Reaney wrote in his Editorial to the first number of *Alphabet*. "Metaphors seemed lies. Poetry seemed to have no use at all. The moon looked enchanting through the trees on Charles Street, but the enchantment was really nothing but an illusion of clouds and fantasy covering up a hideous pock-marked spherical desert. When I told this part of my problem to my friend, he showed me a passage from the *Marriage of Heaven and Hell* which had the effect of starting me back to the belief I had held as a child that metaphor is reality." The particular passage was the Devil's reply to the Angel: "All that we saw was owing to your metaphysics." What they had seen was the head of Leviathan in the fiery pit which the Angel declared to be the Devil's "eternal lot." As soon as the Angel left the pit, however, the Devil found himself sitting by moonlight on a pleasant bank of a river listening to a harper sing about the reptiles bred in the mind of the man who never alters his opinions. Leviathan, in other words, is the reptile bred by an Angel's fixed mind.

Reaney's conversation with his friend is recreated in part in the March eclogue of *A Suit of Nettles* in which Branwell sings a song of Experience and Effie replies with a song of Innocence. Branwell, echoing Reaney to his friend, dreams he is surrounded by moons, "all twenty-eight silvery pock-faced whores," and that life sub-lunar is but various forms of a single rat. Effie, echoing Reaney's Blakean friend, replies to Branwell by suggesting that his demonic vision is simply the unimaginative form of her own Paradisal one. "And of my piping child you are the fallen heir," she assures him.

In *The Red Heart*, Branwell is far more in evidence than Effie; the song that Reaney sings is primarily a song of Experience. But, as Milton Wilson has argued in his review of *A Suit of Nettles* in *Canadian Forum* (October, 1958), Reaney's first volume of poetry "shows an engaging mythological innocence." Unlike Blake, whose influence was to be in all respects transforming, Reaney (in *The Red Heart*) had no sense of "Contraries" interacting to produce a higher innocence. For this reason, it is his most inert volume of poetry. He himself was barely aware of any pattern holding it together; he collected poems he considered worth preserving or revising, wrote others and left it to Colleen Thibaudeau and Sybil Hutchison to work out an arrangement. "Mr. Reaney," commented E.K. Brown in reviewing the volume in *UTQ* (July, 1949) "appears to be vulnerable to boredom beyond any other Canadian who has taken to writing."

"Part of the predicament I am about to describe is that no one seems to know, no one seems to be able to tell you, whether you should be self-conscious or unconscious about the craft of poetry, whether you should really tackle literary criticism as a help or intuitively arrive at the same goal," Reaney wrote in "The Canadian Poet's Predicament" in 1957. Reaney in *The Red Heart* was largely unconscious of his craft; he had not as yet tackled literary criticism, nor had he arrived intuitively "at the same goal" that Frye had. Yet, despite the absence of self-consciousness and the evident absence of a goal, there are, in the volume, certain recurrent images and *motifs* that suggest a pattern upon which he would later build.

E.K. Brown, who was struck by Reaney's ennui, argued that the only break-through in *The Red Heart* came from something dropping. "The droppings from the sky have intensity, but what their significance may be, the poems do not suggest," he concluded. Clearly, however, Professor Brown was wrong: the poems do suggest the significance of the "droppings," though the degree of deliberateness on Reaney's part can only be guessed at. The droppings suggest the Antichrist, who in *The Red Heart* is a dead child presiding in a ghostly manner over an annihilated world. Branwell, whose song of Experience in the March eclogue picks up much of the imagery of *The Red Heart*, is, as Effie points out, "the fallen heir" of her "piping child" or imagination. The controlling theme, though somewhat unfocussed, in *The Red Heart* is the death of the imagination whose symbol is the child. Antichrist is the accusing prince of darkness who puts out the sun, the planets, the human heart, and ultimately time itself.

When Professor Brown wrote of Reaney's ennui and bore-dom he was again wrong. Reaney, as has been demonstrated, received his early imaginative education in the apolcalyptic school of the "new sects of the Protestant Left." The world in which he imaginatively lived as a child was populated by Devils, and Antichrist as a result was no stranger to his dreams. During the years of the Second World War, it was, in the evangelical world that Reaney knew, common knowledge that Hitler was the Anti-Christ (hence the Hitler mask of the Antichrist child in *Colours in the Dark*) and that the end of the world, in some form or other, was at hand. "Immediately after the tribulation of those days shall the sun be darkened, and the moon shall not give her light, and the stars shall fall from the heaven, and the powers of the heavens shall be shaken."

Reaney in *The Red Heart* has not abandoned the apocalyptic world he knew as a child; what he has done is to convert it into an image of the end of childhood, which for those who believe in the reality of metaphor *is* the end of the world. The apocalyptic fireworks attendant upon the descriptions of the end in the gospels and, above all, in Revelations, have been radically muted in *The Red Heart*. What is communicated in such poems as "The Plum Tree" and "The School Globe" is the unearthly sinister stillness of a world put out in which a single child is the sole survivor. In "The Plum Tree" that world is a "lonely haunted farmhouse"; in "The School Globe" it is an "empty schoolroom."

The unique quality of many of his lyrics, filled with a Wordsworthian nostalgia and sense of loss, is the very un-Wordsworthian identification of the child with Antichrist. Wordsworth suggested such an identification on one or two oc-casions in his poetry; in the "Intimations Ode," for example ("Nutting" would be another), he described the growing boy surrounded by prison-house shades, no longer apparelled in "celestial light." The latter phrase comes from Satan's speech in the presence of Bellzebub in the first book of *Paradise Lost*; he is contrasting the light of Heaven with the darkness of Hell. While Wordsworth did not pursue the possibilities of a grow-ing child as a fallen Lucifer, his fellow-Romantics (Shelley, Keats, Byron and Blake) made much of the idea, and Reaney, under the influence of Blake, was to perpetuate in his own way this traditional Romantic image. In "Dark Lagoon," for exam-ple, the embryo in the womb of the mother is already being initiated into the world of death, the mother's heart beat being a time-bomb set to go off. In a fine image, the mother's heart is to the embryo

> ...someone who, far away,
> Seemed to be knocking out this epitaph
> With muffled chisel on muffled stone:
> "This child will someday die."

The "name" carved by the "ticking chisel of the monument maker" is the Antichrist: a growing boy holding in his hands the globe of a withered world. In the unrevised version of "The School Globe" (published in *The Undergrad*, November 1946), Reaney wrote:

> He dreamt he held the world
> (A slippery skull within his arms)
> And would not let it go,
> This glazed reticule filled with
> Gold, lead and fire for volcanoes.

The "slippery skull" is the child's dead self, the real world as opposed to the world originally created by the imagination and preserved for Reaney in comic strips such as *Little Orphan Annie* and *The Katzenjammer Kids*. Reaney's Antichrist emerges from the ruins of childhood; his dwelling place is "a hollow sphere/ Filled with torn orchardry." If he is evil, it is not by intention or design; on the contrary he is at a loss to explain his unwilled behaviour. Thus in *The Red Heart* Antichrist as a child is utterly bewildered by the visions of ruin that haunt his dreams:

> He wondered why he more and more
> Dreamed of eclipses of the sun,
> Of sunsets, ruined towns and zeppelins,
> And especially inverted, upside down churches.

One reason that he dreams of them "more and more" is that the poem images Reaney's own childhood in an apocalyptic world, a world which, as he pointed out in his Editorial to the first number of *Alphabet*, was later subjected to the "final clutch of the so-called scientific world." The time-bomb of the heart is thus equated with the time-bomb of the sun. Just as his heart will drag down his body (a "tree of blood") to a forest grave

> ... so the sun shall drag [down]
> Gods, goddesses and parliament buildings,
> Time, Fate, gramaphones and Man.

The image of the body as a "tree of blood" (suggested to Reaney by a purple-veined portrait of Edith Sitwell by Ivan Tchelitchew) is subtly used to image the loss of childhood innocence in "The Top and the String." The vision of delight resides in a wish to be

> ... a spinning top

> Whipped on by a child
> Whose little face was all my sky.

The string that would give him motion belongs to a child's imagination. Instead, however, the speaker is propelled by a "string of blood" which, unlike the child's string, allows for no respite from "passion's bite." The "tree of blood" is the tree of death which, in "The Heart and the Sun," he imaged as "a walking steeple" (with the heart as a red bell tolling within it). Antichrist as a child wonders why he dreams of that steeple as inverted, upside down.

"Antichrist as a Child" is one of the many poems which Reaney revised for *The Red Heart.* Governing all his revisions was a desire to achieve greater clarity and precision. Reaney, however, did not always in this respect trust his own better judgement. The clarity that Reaney was after was less a matter intrinsic to the poems themselves than to the hoped-for audience of readers. The result, as John Sutherland noted in his review of the volume in the *Northern Review* (April-May, 1950), was a sacrifice of horror and contempt for the sake of nostalgia. In clarifying some of his lyrics for the reader, Reaney sacrificed some of their original ambiguity. The original version of "Antichrist as a Child," for example, has a far greater complexity than the revision. The Antichrist, for one thing, is there more a Jamesian apparition than a tangible presence. The sense of wonder in the revised version replaces a pervasive sense of foreboding in which the speaker (the poem was originally written in the first person) assumes the accents of the sly serpent in the garden. Innocence, as such, is absent in the original. In the revised version the Antichrist "crookedly stood/ In his mother's flower garden"; in the original, he crookedly wavered:

> Like the yellow willow-leaf
> Of a crooked candle
> I crookedly waver
> Here in my mother's garden.

In the revised version, his mother "looked so sadly/ Out of an upstairs window at him," in the original version, in addition to looking sadly, she "stares" at the "pale straw star" (Lucifer by daylight, "celestial light" fading "into the light of common day"). In the revised version, "the ugliest weeds/ Avoided his fingers and his touch"; in the original, they in addition, "turn away their pink stars/ Pale as windows recollected in the mind." In the revised version, Reaney wrote:

> And when his shoes began to hurt
> Because his feet were becoming hooves
> He did not let on to anyone
> For fear they would shoot him for a monster.

In the original, something far more sinister is going on:

> Why do my shoes hurt
> Until they bleed but still
> I must not let on to anyone
> About my hooves.
> I must wear shoes
> Or they will shoot me for a monster.

The tendency throughout the revisions in *The Red Heart* is to substitute shoes for hooves as if Reaney, about to appear in public with a first volume of poetry, was himself dressing up for the occasion. As a result the vision in *The Red Heart* loses some of its poisonous bite. Only in the dream visions ("Dream Within Dream"), fantasies ("A Fantasy and a Moral") and the poems which exploit the related Antichrist image of the orphan ("The English Orphan's Monologue," "The Orphanage") does the image of the fallen world emerge with its intended vigour.

Reaney's sense of the demonic is grounded partly in the image of the ticktock heart-sun and partly in a horror of the sting of sex ("cretinous faces" are "the answers/ To those equations/ In ditches and round-shouldered cars"). Like the vision of corruption in *Afternoon Moon* it is more decorative than real, rooted as it is in the arrested world typified by the aesthete, Charles Newburgh. The attempts to soften this vision of decay with a Wordsworthian nostalgia introduce as in "Whither Do You Wander?", a sentimental note that reveals the inadequacy of Reaney's visionary range. Written over a period that overlaps with the composition and revision of *Afternoon Moon*, this first volume of poetry presents in a more objective, less conscious and explicit form the unresolved conflict typified by the relationship between Albert and Charles in *Afternoon Moon*.

While working on his first volume of poetry, Reaney wrote a long poem, "The Dead Rainbow," which he published separately in *Here and Now*. It is a major poem, the most ambitious that Reaney had as yet written, which he considered too obscure, eccentric and complex for inclusion in *The Red Heart*. Had it been included, along with the unrevised forms of such poems as "Antichrist as a Child" and "The School Globe" (both originally published in *The Undergrad*, December, 1947 and November, 1946), "The Heart and the Sun" and "The Katzenjammer Kids" (both originally published in *Contemporary Verse*, Winter, 1947), it would have given to Reaney's first volume a thematic and stylistic unity that the published form lacks.

"The Dead Rainbow" (as opposed to the living rainbow imaging resurrection in *Colours in the Dark*) explores in a brilliantly eccentric tangle of Sitwellian verse, sound, and rhythm patterns the ceaseless turning of "blood and passion's bite." Removing the framing wished-for world of the child in "The Top and the String" whose "little face was all my sky," Reaney brought into full play the corrupt world muted and blunted in "The Red Heart." The seething secret life in the "scrotal city" spawns the "caesars, kaisers, mutes and jackasses" characterizing existence on a planet that is "a mote/In the eye of a star-moted remote/God."

In *The Red Heart* this demonic world, pestilential and evangelic, fails to interact in any organic way with the two other worlds that Reaney constructed: the child's world that lives in memory and the actual world that dissolves it. What clearly is absent is the archetype of the divine child (present in most of his later poetry) to set over against the Antichrist. In Blakean terms, and they were soon to become Reaney's, the Antichrist is an arrested child afraid, like Thel, to leave the garden it has outgrown. Hell, for Blake, is the dungeon constructed by the attempt to preserve the security of the lower Paradise. Reaney's remembered world of childhood in *The Red Heart* is essentially sentimental, a world "of peaceful rest, of pleasant stop." The reality of that world is, again in Blake's terms, "unacted desires." "Sooner murder an infant in its cradle than nurse unacted desires," wrote Blake in his "Proverbs of Hell." The dark world of *The Red Heart*, a world 'writ large' in "The Dead Rainbow," is the unacted desire lurking, like the Satan of Reaney's childhood, in the artificial foliage of an idealized innocence.

For this reason, Reaney's demonic vision is largely limited to the equating of love with lust and therefore of birth with death.

After the orgiastic rite which describes rather too graphically the passion-propelled pestilential journey of the male sperm from the scrotum through the vagina to the Hell-engendered womb, the Angel of Death in "The Dead Rainbow" declares "the cessation of erection/ From the yellow streets of dust/ In the scrotal town of lust." He comes to put an end to obsessive copulation which Reaney, imaging yet again, this time describes in terms of the *danse macabre* supremely realized later in *The Dance of Death at London, Ontario.*

The last section of "The Dead Rainbow" is a Dance of Death seen as a grateful cessation to a nightmare fornication. It is a vision to which Reaney returned in his later poetry exploring it in a larger context than the narrowly sexual one of the early verse. Part of the impact of Blake upon Reaney was his fortunate dissociation of sexuality from the demonic, which in the evangelical world of his childhood and youth had been all too intimately joined. One of the most delightful eclogues of *A Suit of Nettles* deals with a pair of old death-hags who seek to free the barnyard geese of the medieval burden of goose-bearing by introducing them to the most progressive methods of contraception. Wooed by twin brothers they agree to matrimony. On their wedding night they "[tie] the brothers up in sheets of tight/ Glass, beaten gold, cork, rubber, stoppers, sand" and "[lie] back waiting for the sensation/ Of an interesting lively copulaion." The brothers, however, have deliberately chosen these spinsters because they had insulted their "family's sense of lively birth." Imposing upon them "the ripeness of a Nile in bringing forth," the brothers see to it that "the women's loins poured forth a swollen stream."

II

The vision of *The Red Heart* is essentially that of "a sterile land"; in *A Suit of Nettles*, Reaney with "Punch's stick" attempted to "beat fertility" into it. His success can be seen in the "swollen stream" he brought forth: twelve pastoral eclogues, one for each month of the year, modelled on Spenser's *Shepherd's Calendar* with themes and verse forms taken from or reminiscent of it. In "The Dead Rainbow" and some of the poems in *The Red Heart* Reaney in his image of life as a "scrotal town" had ignored the creative aspect of sex that relates it to the larger creative life of the imagination. "The lust of the goat is the bounty of God," wrote Blake in his "Proverbs of

Hell" and it is a bounty that Reaney clearly recognized when with "Punch's stick" he fertilized the wasteland of his early verse. In a class paper for a graduate course in Aesthetics Reaney in 1958 commented: "Northrop Frye is reported to have said in a lecture once that 'art is rooted in the obscene.' Life is certainly rooted in it, physically and mentally; so that what is offensive to modesty may not be offensive to something extremely more important, that is, the imagination."

The mature vision informing *A Suit of Nettles*, Reaney's finest work to date, is partly the result of casting off a false "modesty" whose source is a nightmare vision of sex inherited from evangelical sermons by itinerant preachers with questionable credentials and a penchant for pornography. In that same class paper, Reaney suggested that the "worst obscenities of heathen superstition" were merely "a fumbling imaginative attempt to 'project,' to shape the demonic energies and Augean filthiness of the lower part of one's body somehow or other." The same explanation can be applied to a poem like "The Dead Rainbow," partly because it fails to recognize that in its rejection of the sexual basis of life it also denies the mental and aesthetic. And it is for this reason that in *The Red Heart* Reaney confronted in poem after poem a dead end. "A typical poem from *The Red Heart*," wrote Milton Wilson in *Canadian Forum* (October, 1958), "circles around its subject until Death brings it to a stop, and marionettes, hollyhocks, automobiles, the bosoms of Miss Beatty, Lake Erie, 'all Fire, all Hell, all Poetry, is out.'"

Sexual embrace is the controlling image of "The Dead Rainbow;" it is also the image that Reaney selected to describe the relations between the Muse of Satire and the sterile land in the invocation to *A Suit of Nettles*. Northrop Frye has rightly suggested in his review of the poem (*UTQ*, July, 1959) that a suit of nettles "seems to represent life in the world of Eros or natural love, a mixture of stimulation and discomfort." It is, therefore, associated with the "sting of blood" in *The Red Heart* but, unlike that serpent "sting" it is "goad" that "grows so warm it bursts into blossoms." The phallic "stick" in *The Red Heart*, on the other hand, is "barbarously cut off" from "the vine."

Branwell, who wears the suit of nettles in the poem, suffers, as the embodiment of natural or profane love, all its "stimulation and discomfort." He is the excuse for "more love poems, paradoxes, happy unions, lies." Effie, whose vision of life is mythical and sacramental, is able, with the aid of her imagination, to transcend the limits of Eros and enter the domain of Agape or sacred love. Thus in the December eclogue, Effie willingly goes to the annual slaughter. Aware of the inadequacy of "this cramped stupid goosehouse world," she accepts Death as the "green pathway to the fields of Life." Branwell, on the other hand, wants life. "I can't see a path that leads between one's/ Head & one's body," he tells Effie. Mopsus, the most dynamic goose in the barnyard, moves all the way from a demonic vision of love to a Christian one, having for some of the months, sought a sterile repose in the "ferny groves" of Platonism "where all is bland correct and rational."

Reaney, it can be seen, constructed for his framing vision a version of the four-fold Christian cosmos that defines, or helps to define, the literary tradition connecting Spenser, Shakespeare, Milton and Blake. There is at the top the divine order centred in the Christ-child to which, under Effie's influence, the once Horatian Mopsus is converted:

> A sun, a moon, a crowd of stars,
> A calendar nor clock is he
> By whom I start my year.
> He is most like a sun for he
> Makes his beholders into suns,
> Shadowless and timeless.

Immediately below the divine world is the visionary world presided over by "a piping child" in every respect similar to the piper in Blake's Introduction to his *Songs of Innocence*. This is the world that belongs to Effie's imagination, a world imaging as in a dream the divine one entered by faith. It is, in other words, the poetic counterpart of the religious one. It is, Effie tells Branwell, the "somewhere else" they "seemed to know" in childhood, a dream of "a white walled garden . . / Where a child sat playing on an panpipe," a world whose charms weave a new one and "make spades of swords of war." It is, in other words, the world of "Faerie" in the Spenserian sense of realized human nature. Below this visionary world is the natural world to which man in his fallen or unimaginative condition is bound. It is the world most apparent in *A Suit of Nettles*, the finite cyclic world of nature to which Branwell is committed because, unlike Mopsus, Valancy and Effie, he "can't see a path that leads between one's/ Head & one's body." Branwell, whose suit of nettles changes like the seasons, wants

> . . . offspring summerson autumnman wintersage
> And tricklerrain thawwind panetap upleaf windrage
> Plow and seed and hoe, green, sucklepig, yellowripe
>   sicklestraw and all such glamourie.

Finally, below the realm of nature (including fallen human nature) is the demonic world which seeks to destroy the other three by denying the creative force at work within them. On the natural level, that force is sex which the Mopsus of the first eclogue associates, in the accents of "The Dead Rainbow," with death: "a world of luscious shame/ That into world another funeral lugs." Interestingly and accurately enough, Mopsus identifies this "Jezebel" world with "a dugless wise old anchorite" whose "eyes slide over Bibles slow as slugs." Jezebel, he implies, is born of evangelical sermons that "gelds you from the world." Reaney has here established the equation upon which his early work was constructed. On the visionary level, this force is the imagination which love-sick and love-rejected Branwell rather pathetically lacks. The only world he knows or understands is "the world's hot middle where it's he and she," the world of "feverish stinging clothes." On the divine level, this force is God seen as a divine child whom the Drunken Preacher at Mome Fair comes closest to denying in his demonic Bunuellian version of the Last Supper.

Reaney in *Afternoon Moon* and *The Red Heart* constructed largely at the extremity of vision, partly because he lacked as yet the maturity to confront "the world's hot middle." In *A Suit of Nettles*, on the other hand, he allowed that "hot middle" its due, seeking not to destroy it but to raise it to an imaginative form which is itself the image of a divine one. Branwell is limited to the world of the "scrotal town"; the redeeming virtue of his biological devotion is his refusal to deny one of the natural forms of divine creativity. He cannot, however, make that imaginative leap. "When you are changed then," Effie tells him, "One arm may always remain a goose wing."

The world celebrated in *A Suit of Nettles* is the cyclic one of Spenser's *Mutabilitie Cantos*, a world endlessly begetting and endlessly dying, governed by a principle of order or recurrence like the axle of a turning wheel. Man is born into this world though he does not belong to it; he must therefore either rise above it as Effie, Mopsus and Valancy do, or sink below it as Branwell is forever in danger of doing. Too afraid and too unseeing to remove his suit of brambles, Branwell commits himself to the monotonous round of the wheel of life (imaged for Branwell at the fair as a ferris wheel and a merry-go-round) which Effie with her anagogical focus sees as "a crazed prison/ Of despair."

The cycle of life and death begins in February with the "spirit goslings" descending into the prison house of large goose eggs. In March, Effie reaches "beneath each sitting goose with grace/

and turn[s] their eggs with pleasure on [her] face." Branwell, double-crossed by Dorcas in February (she secretly married George and laid a large egg by him) and momentarily off copulation, asks how she can stand "to midwife scored of cherubs into Hell." Effie replies that her vision of a Paradisal world supports her. The March eclogue, in other words, moves above and below the natural cycle to the visionary and demonic worlds into either of which the natural world is resolved. Without imagination it becomes what Branwell loses an entire spring and summer seeing: "A trapper with a trap of natural laws/ That closes on all animals its starry jaws." With imagination it becomes a fallen world crying out for redemption: the hand of Effie is the hand of "grace."

This redemptive vision is developed in the April eclogue where Valancy (who shares the Christian vision of Mopsus and Effie) and Raymond (committed like Branwell to the natural order) hold a bardic contest in honour of Spring. Raymond (Raymond Knister) speaks of "the arable earth" as a "Black sow goddess huge with birth"; Valancy (Isabella Crawford), on the other hand, raises the sow to a higher order: her limbs "are the rivers of Eden" and her body "a bethlehem." Duncan (Duncan Campbell Scott), who is the judge of the contest, significantly divides the prize between them.

The demonic counterpart of this redemptive vision is treated in various ways in the May and June eclogues. By May, the goslings have been born ("furry bright/ Like infant furry pocket suns"). While dry-nursing the entire flock, Fanny tells Effie of two proponents of contraception who seek to turn their fertile wombs into a "desert barren state." "Can God not damn you for hating being?" the geese inquire. In June, with nature in full blossoming, Branwell has sunk into the depths of melancholy. Parodying Eliot's "The Hollow Men," he sings "I am like a hollow tree/ Dead in the forest of his brothers." The demonic vision, it will be noted, is always treated humorously, until, that is, the last eclogue. December is the "Day of wrath and terror," in which the farmers kill the geese for the Christmas market. Effie, of course, sees in death the resurrection, but it is a resurrection with distinctly ironic overtones. "Who knows." she says, "at the very least we become men/ When we die." The men they at the very least become sit at Christmas dinner "stuffing themselves with two roast geese at least/ And picking their teeth with thin bone from drumsticks." And then the cycle begins again: "a pail of time tipped back into another pail." Keziah, one of the geese that have been saved to perpetuate the race, climbs up in her nest to begin laying.

Transcending this cyclic vision that defines the natural world, there exists, with Effie as its instrument, what Reaney in the December eclogue calls "the waterflames of Love." In these "waterflames" the Christmas celebrants asleep in their beds are drowning. "The waterflames of Love" are, of course, a reference to Christian baptism with its symbolism of spiritual rebirth into a deathless world. The Christmas feast becomes in this context a passover feast. The passover feast, it will be recalled, celebrates the release of the Israelites from the bondage of Egypt. Instructed by Moses, the elders of Israel killed a lamb, dipped a bunch of hyssop in its blood and struck the lintel and two sideposts with it as a sign to the Lord who, seeing it, would passover the door and not allow the Angel of Death to enter. In the December eclogue, the sign over the lintel protecting the Israelites from the Egyptians becomes pink marking rings on the legs of the geese to be saved from slaughter. Effie, who is marked to be saved, gives her ring to Fanny, and Branwell, also marked for salvation, has his stolen by George. In other words, the passover feast in the Old Testament becomes the Christian sacrifice in the New, and Branwell, as a tragic hero, a Christ-figure *manqué*.

The movement of Branwell from the ridiculous melancholic lover of the opening eclogues whose songs parody the 'compliments' of courtly love to the tragic hero within a larger divine comedy suggests something of the scope of Reaney's poem. The irony of Branwell's position as tragic hero is his failure to grasp, as Mopsus and Effie grasp, the interpenetration of the divine pattern of resurrection in the natural pattern of renewal. When Branwell in the March eclogue asks Effie how she can stand "to midwife scores of cherubs into Hell," Effie replies:

If I prevent these eggs from being addled
You must not sneer; this egg may hatch a heart
That will not close itself against a golden dart.

Effie's job is "to midwife scores of cherubs" into a divine world to which this world silently and uncomprehendingly testifies. "A sibyl come to out of her cave she is," declares Mopsus in a moment of extraordinary insight that is the beginning of his conversion. The moment of insight is his recognition that Effie is the doorknob whose job it is to usher men through a door of ignorance into light:

To think by day is half my job,
To size up each approaching hand
And fit it with a surface bland;

I turn as smoothly as I can
To hand of wife and child and man.

In her "curious tale" of the doorknob and door, the doorknob declares that the nature of the door is fundamentally incomprehensible. And it is incomprehensible because the door is that mute, indifferent, blind, impersonal thing to which the universe perceived without imagination is inevitably reduced (Branwell's "pock-marked whore"). To the doorknob, who is the imagination, the door's voice is like "dumb seedless lumps of dark zinc/ When green leaves try on them to think." When the door, convulsed with rage by the presence of the doorknob (like a dead society convulsed with rage by the presence of the poetic imagination), casts it off, it becomes subject to the violent blows of those who wish to get through. The door is eventually smashed and used for firewood while the knob

. . . was toy to children dear,
Still thinking, dreaming, showing them
How to be Ham, Japhet and Shem
And drunken Noah as all men must
Who for the height of being lust.

Leading Mopsus and Branwell out of the "sterile land" is Effie's work of grace and she performs it in part by joining them at Mome Fair in order to explain the merry-go-round, the ferris wheel and the sideshows. Reaney closely links the tale of the doorknob and the door to Mome Fair because both belong to a world of riddle which requires the reader to rouse his heart, belly and mind to "grasp [its] secret alphabet or iconography or language of symbols and myths." Ham, Japhet, Shem and drunken Noah belong to a mythical world which opens the inert door in Effie's parable into an imaginative kingdom. "A grasping such as is involved here," Reaney continued in his Editorial to the first number of *Alphabet*, "leads to a more powerful inner life, or Blake's 'Jerusalem wall.'" Jerusalem's wall is on the other side of that door, and Effie's doorknob sizes up the approaching hands of Branwell and Mopsus and then at Mome Fair turns as smoothly as it can.

What Reaney presents in the September eclogue (the harvest festival both of the poem and of the year) is a variety of ways of ordering experience. On the lowest level is history, the Canadian version of which Reaney describes as a descent into the belly of Leviathan. The vision here, which he associates with Dante's Inferno, is as close to chaos as any vision can be. Beginning with a wanton slaughter of beaver (*Castor grassus*) and ending with an equally wanton slaughter of men (1942), Reaney sees in what he derives from Donald Creighton's *Dominion of the North* only what Ookpik sees in the November eclogue: a God of Death at his winter work. Above history is philosophy, presented by Reaney in terms of the merry-go-round in which the last horse (Heidegger) turns out to be another version of the first horse (Parmenides). Like history, it contains within it no redemptive principle, though insofar as it completes a circular pattern (instead of a linear movement without a purposeful direction) it is more highly structured.

In the ferris wheel, Reaney turns from history and philosophy to myth which brings him closer to the material upon which the vision of *A Suit of Nettles* is based. "When you're on it," Reaney writes of the ferris wheel, "you don't notice this phenomenon [its turning] but by that time you're a clown enjoying your pastime: right now we are learneds and we are enjoying the puzzle of the ferris wheel." Throughout *A Suit of Nettles*, as, argues Reaney, throughout *The Golden Bough*, the ferris wheel has been burning. Caught up in "pastime" (that is, a time that is always passing) readers and actors are barely aware of "this phenomenon." Now Reaney is inviting the reader to become "learned," to step outside the cyclic vision upon which his poem revolves and interpret the puzzle it presents.

Reaney's desire for the reader to grasp the poem's "secret alphabet or iconography or language of symbols and myth" is a request to him to take hold of Effie's doorknob. In terms of the ferris wheel the "sterile land" is seen as the anti-mythical mode of perception, imaged in both the fun house and merry-go-round, which Reaney has been satirizing throughout the poem, particularly in the July and August eclogues. In the August eclogue Reaney attacked the literary criticism of F. R. Leavis (Scrutumnus) who, according to Reaney, preferred "the language of the common sparrow,/ The music of the untaught farrow" to that of the "fancy wren" and "too sweet lark." What, according to Scrutumnus, is admirable about pigs and sparrows is the fact that they sing " 'We copulate,'/ And mean exactly what they state." Reaney's poem is also about copulation, though by it he does not mean only or exactly what some of his geese declare and do.

In the July eclogue, Reaney, with Dr. Hilda Neatby in mind, defended the "reviving curriculum" of Old Strictus against the progressive school of education. After Valancy has listed all the stones "that support New Jerusalem's wall," Anser replies: "My goodness, how useless so far as the actual living of life is con-

reason needed desperately to act it out. If the hero of *Colours in the Dark* is to survive forty days of blackout then he must bring his own colours to it, make himself a world of light in the midst of an actual darkness. Once this fact is recognized, as it obviously is in the later plays, then the fantasy ceases to be fantasy as such and becomes an initiation into genuine life.

This Blakean inversion of good and evil, which Reaney placed at the centre of the Protestant Christian revolutionary tradition, obviously makes considerable demands upon an audience. The dramatic form, as Joyce argued, is one in which the dramatist "presents his image in immediate relation to others." That image in immediate relation to the audience is an image of the Evangelist; what he is requesting of his audience is an imaginative act of re-birth. He wants them to lose the lives they bring with them into the theatre and gain the life his child hero on the stage is projecting.

In his essay, "The Poet and Day-dreaming," Freud argued that the stress which a writer lays on the memories of his childhood "is ultimately derived from the hypothesis that imaginative creation, like day-dreaming, is a continuation of and substitute for the play of childhood." With this notion, Reaney would obviously agree: his whole conception of drama is based upon it. Yet, with Freud's radical separation of the pleasure and reality principles, which relegates works of the imagination to the realm of illusion (if accepted as fiction) or delusion (if accepted as reality), he would not agree. The basis of Reaney's rejection of Freud's view of the imagination as it is expressed in the playworld of the child is rooted not in a psychological but a metaphysical conception of the child. Reaney like Wordsworth views the child essentially as the inhabitant of a divine world whose play activity expresses the radical freedom which characterizes the divine life. The loss of that life is what Reaney means by death, and the imaginative recovery of it through the arts is what he means by eternal life. The weakness of Reaney's early work (*The Red Heart* and *Afternoon Moon*) lies essentially in the absence of this divine dimension in his presentation of childhood. The psychological realism present in his imaging of the end of childhood provides no substantial ground for the demonic world that replaces it. The demonic placed within a purely sentimental vision is in reality a debased form of Gothic melodrama and Reaney, particularly in *Afternoon Moon,* is sometimes guilty of it. Placed, however, within a cosmic framework (as, for example, in *Wuthering Heights*), the Gothic melodrama becomes the outward and visible form of a profound inward reality in the process of discovering itself. Significantly enough,

Reaney in *Listen to the Wind* was consciously recreating the world of the Brontes, and the play itself owes much to his intimate knowledge of his favourite novel, *Wuthering Heights*.

The problem in the early plays, on the other hand, is that the "melodrama" is unfocussed; it is not seen by the audience as a projection, a dreaming out, of the child's world. Harry and his mirror-image, Eli, in *The Killdeer*, Kenneth in *The Easter Egg*, Andy in *The Sun and the Moon* move in an adult world which is throughout most of the play psychically alien and realistically rendered. The colour spectrum projected onto the screen as *Colours in the Dark* advances is but one indication to the audience that the hero's world acted out on the stage is of his own making and reveals therefore the various stages of his psychic growth. That the presentation of these stages in two acts and forty-nine scenes is in no sense linear but moves back and forth in a manner that defies time entirely is yet another indication of where the action projected is really taking place. The hero of *Colours in the Dark* is a hero because he lives in the imagination, the place of heroic action. Like Mopsus in the November eclogue of *A Suit of Nettles*, he is not ruled by "a sun, a moon, a crowd of stars,/ a calendar nor clock"; he is, on the contrary, the sun god himself because Christ "made it what time of year he pleased, changed/ Snow into grass and gave to all such powers." Thus the opening scenes present the hero as the sun as yet unborn into the earth-world. The earth is therefore darkness (the boy is blindfolded by his mother and put to bed with measles) and must remain in darkness until his sun begins to rise, which is to say, until his imagination stirs. The stirrings are the "colours" from a box of crayons in a Planter's Peanut colour book. Because he cannot literally see what is in that book he has to imagine it. And what he imagines is simultaneously the father remembering. The boy in the bed with his colouring book is the father as a child and since "the Child is Father of the Man" what the father is in the present and was in the past is what the child originally "fathered" with his imagination.

In *Listen to the Wind*, Owen and his cousins act out Rider Haggard's incredibly melodramatic novel, *Dawn*, chosen by Reaney because it contained most of the things he himself had been criticized for in his earlier plays. The uses to which that novel are put in the play provide a clear statement of Reaney's conviction that melodrama is essential to any imaginative recreation of the fallen world. "It's a melodrama," Reaney wrote in his Note on *Listen to the Wind*, "but it still affects me very powerfully because the patterns in it are not only sensational but deadly accurate. This *is* a world. Give in to its rules a bit

& you'll find that it guides you out of the abyss we live in a bit more quickly than some dramas I could name. . . . My play is about young people who put on Rider Haggard's *Dawn* because of its strong patterns."

The "strong patterns" of melodrama are, for Reaney, simply the "patterns" of ordinary life which emerge once the veil of familiarity woven by custom, habit and common sense is removed. They are what the real world looks like when subjected to the vision of realized human nature. Owen's mother in the outer play of four unhappy children putting on a play that both enacts their unhappiness and releases them from it is the witch Geraldine of the inner play. In the inner play, *The Saga of Caresfoot Court*, she reveals the visionary or archetypal form of her realistic behaviour in the outer world. The eternal form of Mrs. Taylor, who leaves her husband and her child because she finds in both a world of death, is a demon who kills her unborn child, is haunted by its ghost and spends a guilt-ridden life seeking revenge on its father. A recurrent Jezebel-figure in Reaney's poetry and drama, Geraldine belongs to the tradition of Gothic melodrama: she acts out the demonic dimension present in most ordinary behaviour in the fallen world. By deserting Owen she has physically destroyed him before he has had a chance to live and by committing herself to a lifetime with another man she has acted out her desire for revenge upon her husband's "impotency."

Owen's real purpose in suggesting that he and his three cousins (Branwell Bronte and his three sisters) put on *The Saga of Caresfoot Court* is that the novel was a gift from his father to his mother and a performance of it might bring her back to witness it. She does come back and assume her archetypal role, but like so many adults in the audiences for Reaney's plays she fails to grasp the reality of the visionary world present in the actual one. When the play is over she gets on her husband's horse and leaves. In a brilliantly handled encounter between Owen and his Geraldine-mother at the end of the play, Reaney has Geraldine enact the audience which is about to leave the theatre convinced that it has witnessed a "silly old story" that was, particularly because of the children's improvisations, rather good fun.

When Owen's mother leaves, Owen realizes that the ordinary world cannot fulfill those needs that are essential to life. He decides therefore to change the ending of his play in which the heroine, Angela, dies, to a happy one that images his own desire. Angela is played by Harriet of the outer play and Oliver, from whom she has been brutally separated by her father, is played by Owen. Harriet and Owen are particularly attracted to each other and, despite Owen's illness and their blood relationship, they have discussed the possibility of marriage. Owen decides that marriage shall take place by changing the ending of *The Saga of Caresfoot Court*, that is, by changing the inner rather than the outer world. It is a decision for life rather than death as opposed to a mere wish-fulfillment dream that belongs to the realm of fantasy. Despite what Reaney's critics have argued, Owen now recognizes that "the rules of joy" are not subject to the conventions of naturalism and realism, that the soul has a freedom to choose that defies external circumstances over which one has no control. Thus Reaney's stage direction to the final scene of his miracle play reads: "*The three girl cousins and Owen walk to the front of the stage with three small chairs in their hands which they set down in front of them. Huge shadows are cast behind them. They are free-in Eternity-they will never taste death again.*"

The turning point in Reaney's search for an adequate form for his experimental drama was *Names and Nicknames* in which Reaney succeeded in transforming his entire rural world into the children's game of "Farmer in the Dell." By dreaming it out the children bring reality to a world of appearance and out of that reality make the Real appear. The play ends with "The Betrothal and Christening Feast at Farmer Dell's House." The Christening Feast in the play conquers the demonic power of Old Grandpa Thorntree who, by robbing children of their Christian name and forcing upon them a nickname, sought to take from them the power given to Adam in the original pastoral. The Christening is a return of that power: "Now," wrote Blake in the Argument to *The Marriage of Heaven and Hell*, "is the dominion of Edom, and the return of Adam into Paradise. See Isaiah xxxiv and xxxv chaps."

In this delightful children's play, Reaney first exploited the form adopted, with modifications and variations, in most of the plays he has written since (*The Three Desks* is an unfortunate exception). The actors first line up before the audience and tell the audience who they are in real life and who they are in the play. There follows a discussion of names and nicknames in which the audience is invited to participate: "How many in the audience ever had a nickname? How many liked their nickname?" The chorus of children then announces the first scene: "The farm in the morning. The Farm: Farmer Dell's Farm." This scene begins with word lists from *The Practical Speller* thrown back and forth by the chorus and invoking the farm's setting. Then the chorus picks up the barnyard sounds, a rooster crowing, a cow mooing, milking sounds, the sound of a cream separator, a bird whistling, crows cawing, frogs croaking ("Knee deep Knee deep Knee deep"). As the play moves through the seasonal cycle of rural life, the chorus assumes the roles of various barnyard animals. When, for example, Cousin Etta sprinkles feed for the chickens, the chorus runs and picks it up "making hen cackles and other chicken noises that come to hand." In the autumn sequence it imitates the whistling sound of the wind. This sound continues while under it half the chorus recites an autumn lyric which slowly shifts its sound and rhythm patterns to suggest the gradual cessation of all movement and the settling in of winter:

> The stream is still with
> The stream is still with
> Still still still still
> Ice ice ice ice
> Oh

"4 years ago [a year after Reaney saw the *Peking National Opera* in which gestures and mime took the place of props and sets] John Hirsch directed a children's play of mine called *Names and Nicknames* at the *Manitoba Theatre Centre*," Reaney wrote in his Note to *Listen to the Wind*. "With a dozen children, six young actors (among them Martha Henry and Heath Lambert) & words taken from my father's old *Practical Speller*, John Hirsch created a magic hour that has remained with me ever since. The simpler art is–the richer it is. Words, gestures & a few rhythm band instruments create a world that turns Cinerama around & makes you the movie projector." From this play and this performance Reaney dates the beginning of a kind of drama in which for the first time he found a form and technique adequate to the kind of poetic vision he wished to endow with a genuine theatrical life of its own. For the first time he was free to break radically with many of the conventions of the so-called well-made play which inhibited and distorted the kind of world he was attempting to create. *Listen to the Wind*, in which the chorus assumes all the functions first opened up in *Names and Nicknames*, is an attempt to apply the dramatic techniques of Reaney's children's play to material and to a subject likely to more immediately attract an adult audience. In *Colours in the Dark* an elaborate system of back projection upon five screens in the form of a cross assumes some of the roles which Reaney invented for a chorus. The result was perhaps a certain imbalance between Reaney's play and the production it was given. It yet remains to be seen whether Reaney's notion that "the simpler art is–the richer it is" is one that can survive the kind of production that Stratford is famous for. Reaney is clearly destined to be the first Canadian playwright to gain international recognition because of the Stratford Festival. Indeed, as Herbert Whittaker has suggested in his review of *Colours in the Dark* in the *Globe and Mail* (July 26, 1967) it may yet turn out that the Stratford Festival theatre will be remembered for Reaney rather than Shakespeare. Should this prove to be the case the conventions of the Shakespearean stage modified and up-dated by Tyrone Guthrie and Michael Langham may give way to conventions resembling those of the *Peking National Opera*.

Reaney's recent work with the *Listener's Workshop* at the now defunct *Alpha Centre* is a far cry, despite the similarity of the underlying conception, from the John Hirsch production of *Colours in the Dark*. The Festival and Avon theatre stages bear little resemblance to the "bare, long room up above a store," that Reaney recommended for the performance of Canadian plays in his Editorial in *Alphabet*. One must, of course, place Reaney's recommendation in its characteristic Reaney context. In Reaney's imagination there is a non-stop mock heroic performance taking place. The more serious he is as a Canadian artist (as distinct from any other kind) the more likely he is to remain close to a barnyard full of Canadian geese. "The bare, long room above a store" is another version of that barnyard and so long as the illusion of it can be preserved Reaney will probably be satisfied that he is on recognizable "home" ground. Reaney's berrypickers and endless line of children belonging to the local storekeeper never reached the stage in *The Rules of Joy* partly because they were trapped mid-Atlantic between Elizabethan rustics tailor-made for a Shakespearean stage and native grown Canadian geese. Reaney has now managed that hurdle with considerable ease. Ahead of him lies at his disposal an international audience, one of the world's finest theatres, and a company of actors matched only by the *Moscow Arts Theatre*, the *Berliner Ensemble*, the *Royal Shakespeare Company* and the *National Theatre* of England. It will require considerable dramatic ingenuity to preserve in such a setting and in such a company the identity of his barnyard geese. Since, however, it survived exposure to Spenser and the epic grandeur of the four-fold Christian cosmos its chances of survival at Stratford appear altogether likely.

SELECTED BIBLIOGRAPHY

PRIMARY SOURCES

BOOKS OF POETRY
The Dance of Death at London, Ontario. Drawings by Jack
    Chambers. London, Ontario. Alphabet Press, 1963.
The Red Heart ("Indian File No. 3"). Toronto: McClelland &
    Stewart, 1949.
A Suit of Nettles. Toronto: Macmillan of Canada, 1958.
Twelve Letters to a Small Town. Toronto: The Ryerson Press, 1962.

INDIVIDUAL POEMS
(listed under journals, magazines, anthologies in which they first
appeared)
Alphabet
"The Alphabet" (September, 1960).
Atlantic Monthly
"Starling with a Split Tongue" (November, 1964);
"The Sun" (February, 1965).
Canadian Forum
"To the Avon River Above Stratford, Canada" (February, 1951);
"A Domestic Song Cycle" (August, 1959);
"Doomsday on the Red-Headed Woodpecker" (July, 1962);
"The Executioner of Mary Stuart" (May, 1962);
"Gray Pillar" (April, 1948);
"Green Glass" (May, 1948);
"Klaxon" (April, 1948);
"Monologue (Spoken by an orphan servant-girl)" (June, 1948);
"Night Train" (May, 1948);
"Rachel" (March, 1962);
"The Sundogs" (June, 1948);
"The Tall Black Hat" (August, 1952).
Canadian Poetry Magazine
"!!Warning!!" (September, 1947);
"The Death of the Poetess" (December, 1947);
"Rewards for Ambitious Trees" (December, 1947).
Contemporary Verse
"Childhood Musette" (Winter, 1947-1948);
"The Death of the Poet" (Summer, 1947);
"Gunpowder Plot" (Summer, 1951);
"The Heart and the Sun" (Winter, 1947-1948);
"The Katzenjammer Kids" (Winter, 1947-1948);
"Lake Ontario" (Fall, 1948);
"Madame Moth" (Fall, 1948);
"Pink and White Hollyhocks" (Summer, 1947);
"Platonic Love" (Winter, 1949-1950);
"The Rape of the Somnambulist" (Winter, 1947-1948);

"A Song for the Suns" (Fall, 1948);
"Winter's Tales" (Winter, 1949-1950).
Driftwood
"Quaker Ninth but Roman Eleventh" (Fall, 1945).
Here and Now
"The Dead Rainbow" (May, 1948);
"The Birth of Venus" (December, 1947).
The Literary Review
"Gifts" (Summer, 1965);
"The Killdeer" (Summer, 1965).
Northern Review
"The Antiquary" (July-Augut, 1948);
"The Bird of Paradise" (August-September, 1949);
"The Canadian" (December-January, 1949-1950);
"Childhood Musette" (July-August, 1948) - a different poem from
    the one with the same title published in *Contemporary Verse;*
"The Groats" (July-August, 1948);
"In This Round Place" (October-November, 1951);
"The Mysterious Rose Garden" (July-August, 1948);
"The Table of Dishes" (April-May, 1953).
Other Canadians: An Anthology of the New Poetry in Canada, 1940-
    1946, ed. John Sutherland. Montreal: First Statement Press,
    1947.
"The Gramaphone";
"Mrs. Wentworth".
Poetry (Chicago)
"A Cellar Song" (September, 1959);
"The Windyard" (September, 1959).
Poetry 62, ed. Eli Mandel and Jean-Guy Pilon. Toronto: The
    Ryerson Press, 1961.
"A Message to Winnipeg."
Quarry Fourteen, ed. Tom Eadie, Kingston, Ontario: The Quarry
    Press, 1965.
"The Stoneboat."
Queen's Quarterly
"The Baby" (Summer, 1959);
"The Horn" (Spring, 1954).
The Tamarack Review
"The April & May Eclogues" (Spring, 1957).
The Undergrad
"Antichrist as a Child" (1946-1947);
"Decadence" (1946-1947);
"Faces and the Drama in a Cup of Tea" (1946);
"The Ivory Steeple" (1948);
"The Kites" (1946-1947);
"Kodak" (1946);
"Miss MacPherson's Letters" (1946-1947);
". . . 1932" (1946-1947);
"The Orphanage" (1946-1947);
"The School Globe" (1946);

"Some New Imaginary Conversations and Soliloquies" (1948);
"The Trojan Horse" (1946-1947);
"The Wicked Streets" (1946).
The Varsity
"The Thunderstorm" (January 18, 1960).
The Varsity Chapbook, ed. John Robert Colombo. Toronto: The
    Ryerson Press, 1959.
"The Man Hunter."
The Waterloo Review
"To Bishop Berkeley" (Winter, 1961);
"The Dwarf" (Summer, 1960);
"This Page" (Spring, 1958);
"Writing & Loving" (Spring, 1958).

PROSE SKETCHES AND SHORT STORIES

"Afternoon Moon" (a revised section of an unpublished novel),
    Here and Now, 1 (May, 1948).
"The Book in the Tree," *The Undergrad* (1946-1947).
"The Box Social," *The Undergrad* (1947). Also in *New Liberty
    Magazine*, XXIV (July 19, 1947).
"The Bully," in *Canadian Short Stories*, ed. Robert Weaver and
    Helen James. Toronto: Oxford University Press, 1952. Also in
    Canadian Short Stories, ed. Robert Weaver. ("The World's
    Classics") London: Oxford University Press, 1960.
"Clay Hole," *The Undergrad* (1946).
"Dear Metronome," *Canadian Forum*, XXXII (September, 1952).
"The Elevator," *The Undergrad* (1946).
"Mr. Whur: A Metamorphosis," *Here and Now*, 1 (December,
    1947).
"To the Secret City: From a Winnipeg Sketch-Book," *Queen's
    Quarterly* LXI (Summer, 1954).
"The Stratford I Remember," *Star Weekly* (August 22, 1959).
"Winnipeg Sketches," *Canadian Forum*, XXXXV (November,
    1955).
"The Young Necrophiles," *Canadian Forum*, XXVIII (September,
    1948).

ARTICLES AND RELATED WORKS

*Alphabet: A Semiannual Devoted to the Iconography of the
    Imagination*. ed. James Reaney. 270 Huron Street, London,
    Ontario: The Alphabet Press.
"Another View of the Writers' Conference," *Canadian Forum*,
    XXXV (October, 1965).
The Boy With an R in His Hand. Toronto: Macmillan of Canada,
    1965.
"The Canadian Imagination," *Poetry* (Chicago), XCIV (June,
    1959).
"The Canadian Poet's Predicament," *UTQ*, XXVI (April, 1957).
    Also *Masks of Poetry: Canadian Critics on Canadian Verse*, ed.
    A.J.M. Smith. Toronto: McClelland and Stewart, 1962.

"The Conditions of Light: Henry James's *The Sacred Fount*,"
  UTQ, XXXI (January, 1962).
"Edith Sitwell's Early Poetry, or Miss Sitwell's Early Poetry," *The
  Undergrad* (March, 1948).
"E.J. Pratt: The Dragonslayer," in *Great Canadians*, ed. Pierre
  Berton and others. Toronto: The Canadian Centennial
  Publishing Company, 1965.
"An Evening with Babble and Doodle: Presentations of
  Poetry,"
  Canadian Literature, XII (Spring, 1962).
"Isabella Valancy Crawford," in *Our Living Tradition: Second and
  Third Series*, ed. Robert L. McDougall. Toronto: University
  of Toronto Press, 1959.
"The Novels of Ivy Compton-Burnett," *Canadian Forum*, XXIX
  (April, 1949).
"The Plays at Stratford," *Canadian Forum*, XXXIII (September,
  1953).
"Search for an Undiscovered Alphabet," *Canadian Art*, XCII
  (September-October, 1965).
"The Stratford Festival," *Canadian Forum*, XXXIII (August,
  1953).
"Ten Miles High on a Song," *The Globe Magazine* (December 24,
  1966).
"Ten Years at Play," *Canadian Literature*, XLI (Summer, 1969).
"The Third Eye: Jay MacPherson's *The Boatman*," *Canadian
  Literature*, II (Winter, 1960). Also in *A Choice of Critics:
  Essays from Canadian Literature*, ed. George Woodcock.
  Toronto: Oxford University Press, 1966.
"Towards the Last Spike: the Treatment of a Western Subject,"
  Northern Review, VII (Summer, 1955).
"Writing," *Journal of the Royal Architectural Institute of Canada*,
  XXXVII (April, 1960).

DRAMATIC WRITING AND WORKS FOR RADIO
Published
Colours in the Dark. Vancouver: Talonplays with Macmillan of
  Canada, 1969.
The Killdeer & Other Plays (*The Killdeer, The Sun and the Moon,
  One-Man Masque, Night Blooming Cereus*). Toronto:
  Macmillan of Canada, 1962.
Let's Make a Carol: A Play with Music for children. Story and
  libretto by James Reaney, music by Alfred Kinz. Waterloo,
  Ontario: Waterloo Music Company, 1965.
Listen to the Wind. Vancouver: Talonplays with Macmillan of
  Canada, 1971.
Names & Nicknames & Other Plays for Young People. Vancouver:
  Talonplays with Macmillan of Canada, 1972.
Unpublished
The Bacchae (translation of Euripides' tragedy)
Part 1, *Canada Dash, Canada Dot: The Line Across*. Music by John

Beckwith. Produced on CBC Radio, November, 1965.

Part II, *Canada Dash, Canada Dot: The Line Up and Down.* Music by John Beckwith. Produced on CBC Radio, December 1966.

Part III, *Canada Dot.* Music by John Beckwith. Produced on CBC Radio, November, 1967.

The Canada Tree. First performance: Girl Guide Heritage Camp, Morrison Island, Ontario, July, 1967.

The Easter Egg

Don't Sell Mr. Aesop. First Performance: Grand Theatre, London, Ontario, December 28, 1967.

Genesis. First Performance: Alpha Centre, London, Ontario, June 1, 1968.

Geography Match. First Performance: Middlesex College Theatre, May 19, 1967.

Ignoramus. First performance: Second Theatre, Dixon Building, London, Ontario, December 27, 1966.

The Journals & Letters of William Blake, (Radio talk). Read on CBC Wednesday Night, April, 1961.

Poet and City - Winnipeg. Music by John Beckwith. Produced on CBC Wednesday Night, September, 1960.

The Revenger's Tragedie by Cyril Tourneur. An adaptation by James Reaney for CBC Wednesday Night, but never produced and broadcast.

The Shivaree (libretto of an opera)

The Three Desks. First performance: Grand Theatre, London, Ontario, February 3, 1967.

Wednesday's Child. Music by John Beckwith. Produced on CBC Wednesday Night, December 5, 1962.

SECONDARY SOURCES

BOOKS, ARTICLES AND SELECTED REVIEWS

Avison, Margaret. "Poetry in Canada," *Poetry* (Chicago), XCIV (June, 1959), pp. 182-5.

Bowering, George. "Why James Reaney is a Better Poet," *Canadian Literature* (Spring, 1968), pp. 40-9.

Brown, E. K.: "Letters in Canada: 1949," *UTQ*, XIX (1950), pp. 262-3 (review of *Red Heart*).

Colombo, J. R. "Antichrist as a Child," *The Varsity* (January 18, 1960), pp.4-5 (interview with Reaney).

Darlington, W. A. "In Search of a Roost," *Daily Telegraph* (London, England), May 6, 1963 (review of *The Killdeer & Other Plays*).

Frye, Northrop. "Letters in Canada: 1958," *UTQ*, XXXVII (July, 1959), pp. 345-8 (review of *A Suit of Nettles*).

Klinck, C. F. (general ed.) *Literary History of Canada: Canadian Literature in English.* Toronto: University of Toronto Press (1965), pp. 648-9.

Lee, A. A. *James Reaney*. New York: Twayne Publishers Inc., 1969.

      "A Turn to the Stage: Reaney's Dramatic Verse," *Canadian Literature*, XV-XVI (Winter & Spring, 1963), pp. 40-51.

MacPherson, Jay. "Listen to the Wind," *Canadian Forum*, XLVI (September, 1966), pp. 136-7.

Mandel, Eli. Review of *A Suit of Nettles, Dalhousie Review*, XXXIX (Summer, 1959), pp. 262-4.

Moore, Mavor. "This Play May Become Part of Our History,"*Toronto Telegram*, January 27, 1960 (review of *The Killdeer*).

Pacey, Desmond. "The Poetry of the Last Thirty Years," *Creative Writing in Canada*. Toronto: The Ryerson Press, 1951, pp. 154-6.

Sutherland, John. "Canadian Comment," *Northern Review*, III (April, May, 1950), pp. 36-42 (review of *The Red Heart*).

Sylvestre, Guy; Conron, Brandon and Klinck, C. F. (eds.) *Canadian Writers/Ecrivains Canadiens: A Biographical Dictionary*. Toronto: The Ryerson Press, 1964, pp. 113

Tait, Michael. "The Limits of Innocence: James Reaney's Theatre," *Canadian Literature*, XIX (Winter, 1964), pp. 43-8.

Wilson, Milton. "On Reviewing Reaney," *The Tamarack Review*, XXVI (Winter, 1963), pp. 71-8 (reviews of *The Killdeer* and *Twelve Letters to a Small Town*).

      "Turning New Leaves," *Canadian Forum*, XXXVIII, (October, 1958), pp. 160-2 (review of *A Suit of Nettles*).

ACKNOWLEDGEMENTS

I am indebted to Professors Richard Stingle and Clara Thomas for reading the manuscript of this book and offering several valuable suggestions. James Reaney generously placed at my disposal his unpublished manuscripts and his correspondence with John Beckwith and Pamela Terry. Professor Alvin Lee kindly sent me the page-proofs of his book-length study of James Reaney written for Twayne's World Authors Series. His comprehensive bibliography was particularly helpful. Finally, I am grateful to the University of Western Ontario for a summer research grant which assisted me in the preparation of this study.

THE NEW CANADIAN LIBRARY